Developing Science

DEVELOPING SCIENTIFIC SKILLS AND KNOWLEDGE

year

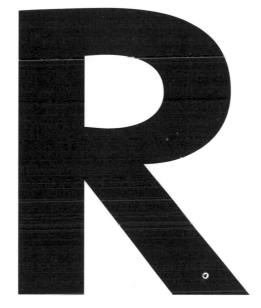

Christine Moorcroft

A & C BLACK

Contents

Materials

Making things work

Published 2003 by A & C Black Publishers Limited
37 Soho Square, London W1D 3QZ
www.acblack.com

ISBN 0-7136-6639-0

Copyright text © Christine Moorcroft, 2003
Copyright illustrations © Gaynor Berry, 2003
Copyright cover illustration © Kay Widdowson, 2003
Editor: Jane Klima
Design: Susan McIntyre

The author and publishers would like to thank Catherine
Yemm, Trevor Davies and the staff of Balsall Common Primary
School for their assistance in producing this series of books.

A CIP catalogue record for this book is available from the
British Library.

Printed in Great Britain by St Edmundsbury Press Ltd,
Bury St Edmunds, Suffolk.

A & C Black uses paper produced with elemental chlorine-
free pulp, harvested from managed sustainable forests.

Introduction

Developing Science is a series of seven photocopiable activity books for science lessons. Each book provides a range of activities that not only develop children's knowledge and understanding of science, but also provide opportunities to develop their scientific skills: planning experimental work, and obtaining and considering evidence. Where appropriate, the activities are linked to other subjects.

The activities vary in their approach: some are based on children's first-hand observations, some present the findings of investigations for the children to analyse and others require the children to find information from books and electronic sources. They focus on different parts of a scientific investigation: questioning, responding to questions, generating ideas, planning, predicting, carrying out a fair test or an investigation, recording findings, checking and questioning findings, explaining findings and presenting explanations.

The activities in **Year R** are based on *Curriculum guidance for the foundation stage: Knowledge and understanding of the world*, which lays the foundations for the science objectives in Key Stage 1 and provides opportunities for the children to:
- ask questions about why things happen;
- investigate a variety of objects and materials in the natural and made world;
- learn about themselves and living things;
- look closely at similarities and differences, patterns and change;
- talk about and record their observations.

The activities will also help children to work towards other learning goals set out in *Curriculum guidance for the foundation stage*. For details, see the notes on pages 5–11.

Teachers are encouraged to introduce the activities presented in this book in a stimulating classroom environment that provides facilities for the children to explore, through play, using movement and the senses. For example, you could provide an activity corner where the children can investigate materials, equipment, pictures and books connected with the topics to be covered (such as torches, magnets and wheels), or you could use role play or PE lessons to explore movements (such as the behaviour of springs and the ways animals move). For lower-achieving children, many of the activities can be completed as a group activity led by an adult. In all activities the children will be more likely to succeed if they have first handled, or observed, and discussed the materials and equipment.

Each activity sheet specifies the learning objective and has a **Teachers' note** at the foot of the page. Expanded teaching notes are provided in **Notes on the activities** on pages 5–11. Most activity sheets also end with a challenge (**Now try this!**), which reinforces and extends the children's learning and provides the teacher with an opportunity for assessment. These more challenging activities might be appropriate for only a few children; it is not expected that the whole class should complete them. A notebook or separate sheet of paper will be required for the children to complete the extension activities, or they could use the back of the activity sheet itself.

Organisation

The activities require very few resources beyond pencils, scissors, card, blocks and other general classroom items. Other materials are specified in the **Notes on the activities** (for example, magnifying glasses, toy cars and information books on specific topics).

Health and safety

Developing Science recognises the importance of safety in science lessons and provides advice on the ways in which teachers can make their lessons as safe as possible (including links to useful websites). The books also suggest ways in which to encourage children to take appropriate responsibility for their own safety. Teachers are recommended to follow the safety guidelines provided in the QCA scheme of work or in *Be Safe!* (available from the Association for Science Education). Specific health and safety advice is included in the **Notes on the activities** and warnings to the children feature on the activity sheets where relevant.

Reading

Most children will be able to carry out the activities independently. It is not expected that the children should be able to read all the instructions on the sheets, but that someone will read them with them. Children gradually become accustomed to seeing instructions, and learn their purpose long before they can read them.

Vocabulary

Vocabulary to be introduced is provided in the **Notes on the activities**, to contribute to the children's skills in *Communication, language and literacy*.

Online resources

In addition to the photocopiable activity sheets in this book, a collection of online science resources is available on the A & C Black website at www.acblack.com/developingscience. These activities can be used either as stand-alone teaching resources or in conjunction with the printed sheets. An **ICT** icon on an activity page indicates that there is a resource on the website specifically designed to complement that activity.

To enable them to be used by children of a wide range of abilities, all of the activities on the website feature both written and spoken instructions. The tasks have been designed to provide experiences that are not easy to reproduce in the classroom: for example, children can investigate a host of different sounds, see a video clip that shows how an animal moves, or closely examine detailed colour photographs of many plants and flowers.

Notes on the activities

The notes below expand upon those provided at the foot of the activity pages. They give ideas for making the most of the activity sheet, including suggestions for the whole-class introduction and discussion or for follow-up work using an adapted version of the sheet. To help teachers to select appropriate learning experiences for their pupils, the activities are grouped into sections within each book, but the pages need not be presented in the order in which they appear unless stated otherwise.

All about me

This is me! (page 12) could be introduced through a song in which the children have to point to parts of their bodies, such as *Put your finger on your head*, *Heads and shoulders, knees and toes* or *Nicky, knacky, knocky, noo* (from *Okki-Tokki-Unga*, A & C Black). Ask them how many arms, heads, knees, legs, shoulders, hands, feet they have. The children could draw round the outline of one of the class and add details. Help them to write labels and to link them to the appropriate parts of the picture. This sheet relates to objectives in the curriculum areas of *Creative development* (Begin to build a repertoire of songs) and *Personal, social and emotional development* (Have a positive self-image).

> **Vocabulary:** *arm, hand, head, foot, leg.*

We are all the same (page 13) focuses on the similarities between people and follows on from page 12. Ask two children to stand in front of the group and the others to say how they are alike. Ask questions to help them to begin: for example, 'Do they both have eyes?', 'Do they both have fingers?', 'Do they both have ears?' Repeat the activity with a child and a picture of an animal: 'Do they both have feathers?', 'Do they both have fur?' The children could ask questions of their own. This activity links up with objectives in *Communication, language and literacy* (Extend vocabulary) and *Creative development* (Make comparisons).

> **Vocabulary:** *arms, claws, face, feet, fins, hands, hooves, horns, legs, paws, tail, wings.*

We are all different (page 14) focuses on the differences between people – the features that make us unique. Start with a fun activity: cut a hole in a large piece of fabric and ask the children to take turns to put their faces through the hole. The others must say who it is and how they can tell. Draw attention to the characteristic features of each child by which he or she can be recognised. This would not be suitable if any child has a birthmark or other feature to which he or she would not want attention drawn. This sheet could be connected with work in *Communication, language and literacy* (Extend vocabulary), in *Mathematical development* (Begin to talk about the shapes of everyday objects) and in *Creative development* (Make comparisons).

> **Vocabulary:** *chin, ears, eyes, face, hair, mouth, nose.*

Make a face (pages 15 and 16) helps the children to learn the names of facial features and how to recognise them in writing. It could be introduced through an activity song such as *Put your*

finger on your head (from *Okki-Tokki-Unga*, A & C Black). You could introduce the words *left* and *right* and ask the children to point to their right or left eye or ear. These pages relate to work in *Communication, language and literacy* (Extend vocabulary).

> **Vocabulary:** *ear, eye, face, hair, mouth, nose.*

Eye mask (page 17) encourages the children to look closely at and to draw people's eyes. Ask them to talk about what they can see when they look at their

Warn the children not to touch their own or their partner's eyes or to point anything at them (for example, the pencil they are using for drawing).

partner's eyes; they could use a magnifying glass to enhance their observations. During other lessons, the children could cut out pairs of eyes from newspaper or magazine pictures, glue them onto a sheet of paper and draw the rest of the face. They could make 'eye spectacles' by gluing eyes onto old sunglasses (*not* to be worn while walking around). You could use this sheet to complement work in *Communication, language and literacy* (Extend vocabulary).

> **Vocabulary:** *ears, eyebrows, eyelashes, eyes, face, hair, mask, mouth, nose.*

My hands (page 18) could be introduced through finger rhymes such as *Five Little Fingers* by Jack Ouseby, *Finger Play* by Babs Bell Hadjusiewicz or *This Finger's Straight* by Jack Ouseby, all of which are in *Finger Rhymes* (John Foster & Carol Thompson, Oxford University Press). Ask the children about the lengths of their fingers. Which is the shortest and which is the longest? Ask what they can do with their fingers. Provide a magnifying glass or a microscope camera linked to a computer monitor and encourage the children to look closely at their hands. Talk about the names of parts of the hand as seen from the back: *finger, knuckle, nail, thumb*. Give the children who complete the extension activity a word-bank to help them to label their drawings: you could introduce the word *palm*. Encourage them to talk about the lines on their hands and to compare them with those of others in the group. This activity could be linked with work in the area of *Creative development* (Begin to build a repertoire of songs).

> **Vocabulary:** *finger, hand, knuckle, nail, palm, thumb, wrist.*

For **My feet** (page 19) the children will need a magnifying glass or a microscope camera linked to a computer monitor. Invite them to look closely at their feet. Encourage them to talk about the lines and patterns. They could compare their feet with those of a friend. What can they do with their feet? Can they wiggle their toes? Can they move one toe at a time? They could draw and cut out outlines of their feet and compare them with others. Whose feet are the shortest? Who has the longest feet? Who do they think has the biggest shoe size? They could check their answers by looking at the sizes printed in their shoes. Ask the children to count the toes on each foot, and to compare their right and left feet. Are they the same? How are they different? They should notice that the big toe is on the inner side and the little toe is on the outer side. This page could be used in conjunction with work in *Mathematical development* (Count up to ten objects; Use positional language; Use size language).

> **Vocabulary:** *ankle, big, feet, foot, little, sole, toe.*

See how we grow (page 20) could be introduced by showing a collection of photographs of children of different ages. Use the words *young* and *old*, *younger* and *older*. Ask the children to name someone younger than themselves and someone older. How old is the younger person and how old is the older person? Ask the children to choose the oldest and the youngest child and to say how they can tell. They could also bring in photographs of themselves when they were younger. The photographs could be arranged on timelines and labelled with the children's names and their age when each photograph was taken. Ask them how they have changed since they were babies. You could focus on their faces, feet, legs or hands. This activity has links with objectives in *Personal, social and emotional development* (Have a sense of self) and in *Knowledge and understanding of the world* (Remember and talk about significant things that have happened to them).

> **Vocabulary:** *baby, old, older, oldest, young, younger, youngest.*

Things I like (page 21) discusses children's favourite things. Show the children pictures of foods: find out who likes each one; do the same with pictures of drinks. The children could bring in their favourite toy and something in their favourite colour and tell the others what they like about them. They could cut out pictures of foods, drinks, toys and colours they like from magazines, newspapers and catalogues and glue them onto displays labelled *Our favourite foods*, *Our favourite drinks* and so on. This sheet focuses on the areas of *Personal, social and emotional development* (Have a sense of self) and *Knowledge and understanding of the world* (Remember and talk about significant things that have happened to them).

> **Vocabulary:** *best, favourite, like.*

Things I can do (page 22) encourages the children to talk about things people learn to do as they grow up. They could mime the action and describe what they can do. The others could listen and ask questions. Has anyone just learned to do something, such as riding a bike or skipping? You could photograph the children doing these things and present them as a display entitled *We can do it!* This sheet links with work in the areas of *Personal, social and emotional development* (Have a sense of self) and *Communication, language and literacy* (Take turns in conversation; Use talk to relive past experiences).

> **Vocabulary:** *cut, draw, fasten, hop, kick, ride, skip, swim, tie.*

Keeping clean (page 23) focuses on personal hygiene. Ask the children about the times when they wash their hands: for example, when they get up, before eating, before they go to bed, or if their hands get dirty. Ask them if they know what germs are, and explain that they are tiny living things, so tiny that we cannot see them, which can make us ill. Can they name some places where germs might be? Talk about what is happening in the pictures on the activity sheet, and where there might be germs. After the activity, the children could make signs for places in the school where people need to be reminded to wash their hands. You could enact the journey of a germ from one place to

another: make a small picture of a fearsome-looking germ and ask the children to pass it around to show how germs spread from one person's unwashed hands via pencil sharpeners and so on to someone else's mouth and stomach. This page is connected with objectives in the areas of *Personal, social and emotional development* (Value and contribute to their own well-being), *Physical development* (Show awareness of healthy practices) and *Creative development* (Engage in role play; Use one object to represent another).

> **Vocabulary:** *clean, soap, wash, water.*

Using the senses

What can we see? (page 24) focuses on the sense of sight. Ask the children what they see with. Point out the importance of taking care of our eyes and ask them to think about what they should do to avoid accidents to eyes. Tell them, for example, never to point scissors and pencils at anyone's face and to make sure that materials such as sand, flour and sawdust are kept away from eyes. The children might know about the ways in which people protect their eyes from damage (for example, by wearing sunglasses or goggles). They could collect pictures of people at work or leisure using eye protection. The children could close their eyes for ten seconds and imagine what it would be like if they could not see. Point out how important eyesight is, and discuss how people with impaired sight manage everyday activities. You could write to or email the Royal National Institute for the Blind (RNIB) for more information (www.rnib.org). This activity complements work in *Creative development* (Show an interest in what they see, hear, smell, touch and feel; Further explore an experience using a range of senses).

> **Vocabulary:** *blind, eye, eyes, look, see.*

ICT **What can we hear?** (page 25) focuses on the sense of hearing. Ask the children what they hear with. Point out the importance of taking care of our ears and ask them to think about what they should do to avoid damage to ears: for example, they should never put anything in their ears or make loud noises close to anyone's ears. The children might know about the ways in which people protect their ears from damage (for example, by wearing soundproofing earmuffs or earmuffs to keep out the cold). They could collect pictures of people at work or leisure using ear protection. The children could cover their ears while you say something. This would help them to realise that we use our ears to hear sounds and it is difficult when we cannot hear properly. Discuss how people with impaired hearing cope with everyday activities. The children could look at picture books about deafness, for example *I Can't Hear Like You*, by Althea (RNID/Dinosaur). You could end with the action song *Can you hear?* (*Harlequin*, Joan Lawton, A & C Black). This page could be used in conjunction with the area of *Creative development* (Show an interest in what they see, hear, smell, touch and feel; Further explore an experience using a range of senses). A complementary activity for this sheet is available on the website (see Year R Activity 1).

> **Vocabulary:** *deaf, ear, ears, hear, listen.*

Loud or quiet? (page 26) examines contrasting sounds. Ask the children to name any loud sounds they have heard. What is the quietest sound they have heard? You could set up an investigation table of things that make sounds: for example, a doorbell, a handbell, castanets, shakers made from containers of rice, sand or beads, things to scrape (such as a piece of corrugated cardboard or sandpaper glued to a board, with a stick for scraping it), things that crackle (such as cellophane) and things that pop (such as bubble wrap). Talk about the sounds; tell the children the words for the sounds, and ask them to repeat them: *bang, crackle, ring, rustle, scrape, tap*. This activity focuses on the area of *Creative development* (Show an interest in what they see, hear, smell, touch and feel; Further explore an experience using a range of senses).

> **Vocabulary:** *ear, hear, loud, noise, quiet, sound.*

What does it feel like? (page 27) could be linked with work on materials (pages 45–55). Before beginning the activity sheet ask the children to look around the classroom for something soft and something hard. Invite them to talk about the feel of the object. Hold up some objects, let the children feel them, and ask 'Is it soft or hard?' You could set up an investigation table with boxes labelled *soft* and *hard* and invite the children to put things into the correct box. This page could be used in connection with work in *Creative development* (Show an interest in what they see, hear, smell, touch and feel; Further explore an experience using a range of senses).

> **Vocabulary:** *feel, hard, soft, touch.*

Do not touch! (page 28) warns of the dangers of touching some objects. Ask the children about things their parents or carers tell them not to touch. Why should they not touch them? Tell them that some things can harm them because they are hot, or electrical, or sharp, or poisonous, or have germs on them. Ask them to name examples of each. You could make a display entitled *Do not touch!*, to which the children could contribute pictures and writing, or you could make a display of things that are safe to touch and things that are not safe. This sheet relates to work in *Personal, social and emotional development* (Value and contribute to their own well-being).

> **Vocabulary:** *electric, feel, hand, hard, harm, hot, hurt, poison, sharp, skin, soft, touch.*

What can we smell? (page 29) encourages children to associate smells with feelings. Take the children on a 'smelling walk' around the school and its vicinity. What can they smell?

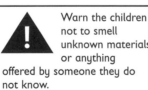

Warn the children not to smell unknown materials or anything offered by someone they do not know.

Ask them if they like the smells and what they remind them of. How do some smells make them feel? (For example, the smell of food cooking might make them feel hungry.) Ask them if they have smelled those smells before and, if so, where. This page focuses on objectives in *Creative development* (Show an interest in what they see, hear, smell, touch and feel; Further explore an experience using a range of senses).

> **Vocabulary:** *nose, smell.*

Use **I like this smell** (page 30) as a follow-up to page 29. Talk about the smells the children found during the 'smelling walk' and ask them about the smells they have smelled in other places: for example, in a supermarket, in a park, in a busy street or on a farm. Which smells do they like? Which ones do they not like? You could use this sheet in connection with *Creative development* (Show an interest in what they see, hear, smell, touch and feel; Further explore an experience using a range of senses).

> **Vocabulary:** *like, nose, smell.*

ICT For **What does it taste like?** (page 31) you will need: some sweet and savoury foods for the children to taste (for example, crisps, savoury and sweet biscuits, slices of banana and other fruits, sweets, honey, bread and yogurt); some pictures of meals (main courses and

Teach the children good food hygiene habits: washing their hands before handling food and always using clean utensils. Check if any of the children suffers from a nut or milk allergy before asking them to taste the foods.

desserts) from magazines or menus; a bag of sugar. Before the children taste any foods, show them how you make sure that everything is clean: cover the table or wash it with an anti-bacterial solution; use utensils that are only for food; use a clean spoon or cocktail stick for each person to pick up foods. Name each food and let the children taste it; ask them if it is sweet. Show the children the pictures of foods and ask them to sort them according to whether or not they are sweet. When do they usually eat sweet things and when do they eat things that are not sweet? Ask them if they know what is in many sweet things. Show them the bag of sugar and explain that sugar can be found in lots of foods. Can they give other examples? This page relates to the curriculum area of *Creative development* (Show an interest in what they see, hear, smell, touch and feel; Further explore an experience using a range of senses). A complementary activity for this sheet is available on the website (see Year R Activity 2).

> **Vocabulary:** *sweet, taste.*

For **My lunch** (page 32) you need three large sheets of paper and some pictures of foods cut from magazines or menus (include several pictures of foods that can be eaten at any meal, such as bread). Ask the children to name their first meal of the day; what other meals do they eat? Write the name of each meal on a separate sheet of paper. Show the children a picture of a food; ask them at which meal they might eat it; ask them to glue it onto the correct sheet. Label the foods. Read the labels with the children. This activity could be linked with work in *Personal, social and emotional development* (Value and contribute to their own well-being).

> **Vocabulary:** *breakfast, dinner, eat, lunch, supper, taste, tea.*

Do not taste! (page 33) helps the children identify the tastes they like and dislike. What is the class's favourite food? Is there a food that is disliked by many of the children? What do they not like about it? Ask them to name some things they should not taste and to say why. Give examples of things that could contain germs, such as foods that have been dropped or licked by animals or other people, or have had flies or other insects on them. Ask the children what they should do if they are offered sweets or other foods, or drinks, by someone they do not know. Point out the dangers of eating or drinking anything from an unlabelled container. You could use this sheet in connection with work in *Personal, social and emotional development* (Value and contribute to their own well-being).

> **Vocabulary:** *danger, no, safe, taste.*

Living things and their environment

Use **Around our school** (page 34) to encourage the children to walk around a park or garden and to look at anything that grows or lives there. Encourage them to look underneath leaves and stones, in the cracks of bark, paths or walls, on the stems of flowers and so on. Can they name the things they see? Tell them the names of any living things they do not know. As far as possible, give the children time to talk about what they observe. Remind the children to replace stones where they found them because they might be an animal's home. This page focuses on *Knowledge and understanding of the world* (Show an interest in the world in which they live).

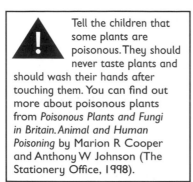

Tell the children that some plants are poisonous. They should never taste plants and should wash their hands after touching them. You can find out more about poisonous plants from *Poisonous Plants and Fungi in Britain. Animal and Human Poisoning* by Marion R Cooper and Anthony W Johnson (The Stationery Office, 1998).

Vocabulary: *butterfly, garden, ladybird, snail, spider, worm.*

ICT For **Leaf match** (page 35), take the children out to collect leaves (or provide a collection of leaves for them to observe). Ask them to sort the leaves into sets of the same kind and encourage them to talk about the similarities and differences between the leaves: their colour, their shape (*long, short, thin, fat*), the number of points, whether they are smooth or rough, shiny or dull, and so on. A complementary activity for this sheet is available on the website (see Year R Activity 3). As an extension activity, the children could sort the collection of leaves according to one criterion, such as size, texture or shape. This page links up with objectives in the areas of *Communication, language and literacy* (Extend vocabulary), *Mathematical development* (Begin to talk about the shapes of everyday objects) and *Creative development* (Make comparisons).

Vocabulary: *garden, jagged, leaf, plant, point, rough, smooth, tree.*

At the park (page 36) involves the children in a visit to a park. Before the outing, ask the children if they have been to a park and what they remember about it. What did they see growing there? Ensure that they understand the word *growing*. What animals did they see there? Which animals live in the park? Which ones were just visiting? You could take a photograph of the park and then go back there with the children at a different time of year and ask them how it has changed. The children could make a miniature park on an old tray filled with potting compost; they could push small sticks, leaves and flowers into the compost and add small stones to create a rock garden. They could make a 'pond' from shiny paper and a path from gravel or matchsticks. This sheet could be related to learning objectives in *Communication, language and literacy* (Extend vocabulary) and *Creative development* (Make comparisons).

Vocabulary: *daffodil, duck, grass, holly, park, rose, sparrow, spider, squirrel, tree, willow.*

ICT **On the beach** (page 37) is about exploring the seaside. Ask the children if they have been to a beach and what they remember about it. What did they see growing there? Ensure that they understand the word *growing*. What animals did they see there? Which animals live on the beach? Which ones were just visiting? Talk about why these animals might be on the beach. How is a beach different from other places and what might the animals like there? The children might enjoy the action poem *Seaside Song* by Tony Mitton (in *Finger Rhymes*, John Foster & Carol Thompson, Oxford University Press). This page focuses on work in *Knowledge and understanding of the world* (Show an interest in the world in which they live). A complementary activity for this sheet is available on the website (see Year R Activity 4).

Vocabulary: *beach, crab, fish, gull, sand, sea, shell, starfish, water.*

Prepare for **At the zoo** (page 38) by talking about why animals are taken from their natural surroundings and placed in zoos or safari parks: so that people can look at them and scientists can study them. If possible, visit a zoo or pets' corner in a park with the children: otherwise show them a video of a zoo and pictures of zoo animals. Ask the children to notice which animals live in or near water and which live on dry land. The children could contribute to a model zoo for which they create a habitat for a given animal (provide them with model zoo animals). You could end the activity by singing *Old MacDonald had a Zoo*! Let each group of children choose a zoo animal to add to the song. This sheet links to the curriculum areas of *Knowledge and understanding of the world* (Show an interest in the world in which they live) and *Creative development* (Begin to build a repertoire of songs).

Vocabulary: *goldfish, land, shark, snake, water, zebra, zoo.*

For **Animal jigsaw** (page 39) first show the children pictures, videos and real-life examples of several animals. Ask them to point out some of the differences between animals: for example, some have legs, some have wings, some have flippers, some have fins, some have tails, some have horns. The children might have to indicate their observations mainly by pointing to the differences in animal pictures: this is an opportunity to introduce new vocabulary. You could play a guessing game in which you give the children clues: for example, 'I am an animal. I have fins. I swim in the sea. Who am I?' This page could be related to work in *Creative development* (Make comparisons).

Vocabulary: *fins, flippers, legs, tail, trotters, wings.*

For **Who is my mum?** (page 40) show the children pictures, videos and real-life examples of animals, their young and their life cycles: for example, in *Minibeasts* by Christine Moorcroft (A & C Black), which also provides a CD of songs and rhymes. Talk about the ways in which animals change as they grow: they get bigger and their bodies change. Ask the children to compare photographs of a caterpillar and a butterfly, a tadpole and a frog, a chick and a hen, and to talk about the differences. You could read stories about animals changing as they grow: for example, *The Very Hungry Caterpillar* by Eric Carle, and poems such as *Caterpillar* by Delphine Evans (in *Finger Rhymes*, John Foster & Carol Thompson, Oxford University Press). This sheet complements work in *Communication, language and literacy* (Extend vocabulary).

Vocabulary: *butterfly, caterpillar, chick, frog, hen, mother, mum, tadpole.*

For **How do they move?** (page 41), show the children pictures, videos and, if possible, real-life examples of several animals, and talk about how the animals move and how their bodies help them to move: for example, many animals that swim have fins, flippers or webbed feet, and animals that run or hop have legs. The children could watch birds in the school grounds. Do they walk or hop? You could introduce the names for any common birds the children can easily recognise, such as bluetit, sparrow and starling; for some children you could change the word *bird* on the activity sheet to *bluetit*, *sparrow* or *starling*, for example. See also page 43. You could use this page in connection with work in *Communication, language and literacy* (Use talk to connect ideas).

> **Vocabulary:** *bird, cat, fly, hop, run, slide, swim, walk, wriggle.*

ICT **What do they eat?** (page 42) talks about the food animals need. You could begin by talking about the things that all animals need, starting with familiar animals such as pets: they all need food, water and shelter. Ask the children about the food eaten by animals they know. Can they think of animals that eat grass, seeds, leaves, meat and so on? They might be able to talk about animals (such as dogs) that eat various foods. You could point out that many animals eat a variety of foods, depending on what they can find. If possible, keep animals such as snails or fish in the classroom for a short time, and let the children observe them feeding. Provide a classroom reference area about animals (include books, pictures and posters, and set up videos for the children to watch). Encourage the children to use the reference library to find out about animals, and show them how to find the information they want. You could talk about this process: for example, 'I want to know about cows, so I'll look at a book called *The Farm*', 'I want to know what dogs eat, so I'll look at this book called *Dogs*'. This could be linked with work in *Communication, language and literacy* (Know that information can be retrieved from books and computers). A complementary activity for this sheet is available on the website (see Year R Activity 5).

> **Vocabulary:** *cat, feed, grass, leaves, meat, seeds.*

A bird (page 43) discusses the activities of all birds. If possible, find a place from which the children can watch birds. You could set up a bird table near to a window to encourage birds to visit the school grounds. Point out that the children will need to be very quiet and as still as possible, so that the birds will not notice them. Ask the children what the birds are doing, and introduce words for the actions: for example, *standing still, feeding, pecking, hopping, walking, running, singing, perching* or *flying*. Encourage the children to use the words you have introduced. The children might enjoy the action poem *The Bird* by Tony Mitton (in *Finger Rhymes*, John Foster & Carol Thompson, Oxford University Press). You could use this page in relation to objectives in *Creative development* (Respond in a variety of ways to what they see and hear) and in *Communication, language and literacy* (Build up vocabulary that reflects the breadth of their experiences).

> **Vocabulary:** *bird, drink, fly, hop, perch, sing, walk.*

ICT **A snail** (page 44) encourages the children to observe snails closely. If possible, bring some snails into school; they can be kept in a plant propagator or aquarium tank lined with soil and stones and some leaves. If they are kept in

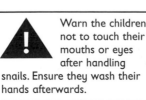

Warn the children not to touch their mouths or eyes after handling snails. Ensure they wash their hands afterwards.

school, ensure that they have a good supply of calcium to keep their shells healthy: mix a teaspoonful of pure calcium carbonate (available from chemists) with three tablespoonfuls of oatmeal and three teaspoonfuls of dried milk, add water to make a thick paste and smear the paste onto the stones in the tank or propagator. Before giving the snails to the children, ask them to think about how to keep the snails safe: draw up 'rules' such as 'Stay seated', 'Make sure the snail cannot fall off the table' and 'Handle the snail gently'. Provide each child with a snail on a piece of clear Perspex, so that they can see the underside of the snail. Can they find its mouth, eyes and feelers? What else do they see? This page connects with work in *Personal, social and emotional development* (Show care for living things). A complementary activity for this sheet is available on the website (see Year R Activity 6).

> **Vocabulary:** *eyes, feelers, foot, head, mouth, shell, slime, snail.*

Materials

For **Sand** (page 45), provide trays of wet and dry sand for the children to explore. As they experiment, ask them what they are doing, and introduce vocabulary as necessary. Talk about what they can and cannot do with wet and dry sand. Ask them to choose which they would use for different purposes: for example, making shapes using a mould, pouring through a sieve, or drawing pictures with their fingers or a stick. Why did they choose dry or wet sand for that purpose? The children could also change the sand: make the dry sand wet and the wet sand dry. Ask them to talk about what they will do and why it will work, before they try out their ideas. Afterwards ask them to describe what they did, what happened and how well it worked. This would link with the area of *Communication, language and literacy* (Use talk to connect ideas and explain what is happening).

> **Vocabulary:** *build, draw, dry, pour, sand, sieve, wet.*

Water (page 46) encourages the children to describe what they can do with water. Provide a water tray or a bowl of water and containers, spoons, scoops and plastic bottles, such as washing-up liquid bottles, for the children to explore. As they experiment, ask them what they are doing, and introduce vocabulary such as *drip, pour, splash, squirt* and *stir*. Talk about other things they do with water, such as *drink, flush, rinse, shower* and *wash*. Stress that they should drink only clean water that they know to be drinking water. This sheet also focuses on work in *Communication, language and literacy* (Use talk to connect ideas and explain what is happening).

> **Vocabulary:** *build, dig, draw, drink, drip, flush, pour, rinse, shower, splash, squirt, stir, wash, water, wet.*

Are they waterproof? (page 47) develops the children's skills in reading and following instructions. They will need to work in groups for this activity. Introduce the word *waterproof* and ask the children if they know what it means. What do they wear that is waterproof? Why do they wear it? You will need collections of gloves (child-sized, if possible) made of plastic, rubber, cotton and wool. This page complements work in *Communication, language and literacy* (Extend vocabulary).

> **Vocabulary:** *bowl, cotton, dry, plastic, rubber, water, waterproof, wet, wool.*

Hot, warm, cold (page 48) introduces children to the idea of different temperatures. Provide some cold and warm things for the children to feel: pots of warm and cold water, stones and bricks that have been left in the sunshine or warmed in an oven, stones and bricks that have been inside a fridge, ice wrapped in a plastic bag, and so on. Ask them if they are warm or cold. Show them pictures of hot things such as electric, gas or solid fuel fires, ovens, boiling kettles, and hot, steaming drinks. Can the children explain why they have been asked to touch only cold and warm things? Talk about the dangers of hot things. You could use this page to complement work in the curriculum areas of *Communication, language and literacy* (Use talk to connect ideas and explain what is happening), *Personal, social and emotional development* (Value and contribute to their own well-being) and *Creative development* (Show an interest in what they see, hear, smell, touch and feel; Further explore an experience using a range of senses).

> **Vocabulary:** *cold, danger, hot, ice, warm.*

Our clothes: 1–4 (pages 49–52) can be used flexibly. Before asking the children to dress the standing figures on page 49, provide a collection of children's clothing and, if possible, a shop dummy for the children to dress for different weather (or you could make a body template out of thick card). You could put an instruction sign next to the dummy: for example, 'Dress Harry for a rainy day'. The figures and clothing on the activity sheets could be coloured in by the children (and then laminated and cut out by an adult) and presented as part of an activity corner that the children can choose to use at different times, rather than having a set for each child. As with the shop dummy, the children could follow instructions about dressing the figures for specific weather. Ask them to show the class the clothes they have chosen and to explain their choices. Discuss the differences between clothes worn in cold, warm and wet weather: the materials, their thickness, the parts of the body they cover, and so on. Discuss other factors affecting the clothes the children wear: for example, where they are and what they are doing. Note that some children (for example, Muslim girls) would keep their legs and arms covered in public whatever the weather. This sheet could be linked with work in *Communication, language and literacy* (Talk activities through, reflecting on and modifying what they are doing).

> **Vocabulary:** *boots, clothes, cold, dry, hat, hood, jacket, jumper, shoes, shorts, skirt, socks, sweatshirt, swimsuit, T-shirt, underwear, warm, wet.*

Rough or smooth? (page 53) presents contrasting textures. Provide a collection of objects for the children to feel; ask them to describe the feel, and introduce the words *rough* and *smooth*. They could look for other rough and smooth things in the classroom: for example, rough mat, smooth whiteboard. This activity relates to objectives in *Creative development* (Show an interest in what they see, hear, smell, touch and feel; Further explore an experience using a range of senses).

> **Vocabulary:** *feel, rough, smooth, touch.*

Squashy stuff (page 54) allows the children to explore materials that change shape. Provide a collection of objects for the children to squash, if they can; ask them which objects are squashy and which are not. Include modelling clay, a cushion or pillow, a sponge, balls, books, bats, pencils, teddy bears and other soft toys, hard wooden or plastic model people or animals, stones and shells. The children could sort the objects into two hoops labelled *squashy* and *not squashy*. They could look for squashy things in the classroom and point out things that are not squashy. This sheet complements work in *Creative development* (Show an interest in what they see, hear, smell, touch and feel; Further explore an experience using a range of senses).

> **Vocabulary:** *press, squash, squashy, squeeze.*

For **Shine on** (page 55), begin with a 'shiny things treasure hunt'. You could give each child a small container such as an ice cream tub in which to collect shiny things from around the school: for example, tin foil, spoons, tinsel, keys, coins, plastic mirrors, glossy paper and plastic and polished metal items. Back in class, invite them to show the others their finds and to talk about them. Talk about the materials from which the shiny things are made. The extension activity could lead to work on mirrors (see page 62); the children could sort the shiny things into two sets: those in which they can or cannot see their reflections. This activity could link up with objectives in *Creative development* (Make collages; Experiment to create different textures).

> **Vocabulary:** *light, mirror, reflection, see, shine, shiny.*

Making things work

Toy cars (page 56) helps the children to investigate how things move. Provide a collection of toy cars for the children to play with. Ask them to explain what makes each car go. They might reply 'the wheels', but ask them how they can make the wheels go round. Place a toy car on the floor and ask the children what they need to do with it to make it move. They could sort the cars according to what makes them move: for example, battery, clockwork, pedal, pull, push. You could use this page to enrich work in the area of *Personal, social and emotional development* (Show curiosity; Show increasing independence in selecting and carrying out activities).

> **Vocabulary:** *battery, car, clockwork, go, pedal, pull, push.*

Boats (page 57) focuses on how things move through water. Show the children videos and pictures of boats that are powered in different ways: sailing boats, rowing boats, motor boats, paddle boats, and so on. Provide model boats powered in different ways (including clockwork and battery) and let them try them out in the water tray. Ask them to notice that when a boat moves, water is also moved. What moves the water? Ask them what makes the boat go; talk about what the people on the boat have to do to make it start moving, to keep it moving, and then to stop it. Show them that all boats except sailboats have something that moves the water: oars, a paddle wheel, or a propeller. This sheet relates to work in *Communication, language and literacy* (Use talk to organise, sequence and clarify thinking).

> **Vocabulary:** *boat, clockwork, motor, oar, paddle, propeller, row, sail, wind.*

Wheels (page 58) could be introduced with the song *The Wheels on the Bus*. You could also set up an investigation table of different artefacts with wheels: toy cars, models, pieces from construction kits, old clocks containing cogs, a steering wheel, and so on. Ask the children to explain what some of the wheels are for and how they are used. They could also make models with wheels using construction materials and recycled materials such as lids, cotton reels and buttons. This activity links up with objectives in *Communication, language and literacy* (Use talk to organise, sequence and clarify thinking) and *Creative development* (Talk about personal intentions, describing what they were trying to do; Make constructions).

Vocabulary: *round, turn, wheel.*

ICT **Turn, turn, turn** (page 59) explores how things with handles work. Provide artefacts that work by turning handles: for example, music

Close supervision is needed.

boxes, tops, whisks and coffee grinders (demonstrate these for safety). The children could watch what happens when they turn the handle; what it turns, what that turns, and so on. Warn them not to put their fingers into any turning mechanisms. This is an opportunity to introduce the safe use of tools such as whisks and drills. You could provide liquids for the children to whisk and set up a thick piece of wood on which they can practise drilling holes. Use a G-clamp to clamp the wood onto a table-top (with another piece under the wood to protect the table). You could use this page to enrich work in the area of *Communication, language and literacy* (Use talk to organise, sequence and clarify thinking). A complementary activity for this sheet is available on the website (see Year R Activity 7).

Vocabulary: *crush, coffee grinder, drill, grind, grip, handle, roundabout, turn, wheel, whisk.*

Music makers (page 60) allows the children to investigate how sounds are produced. Provide a collection of musical instruments for the children to

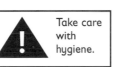
Take care with hygiene.

explore. Ask them what they have to do in order to make a sound. They could sort the instruments into boxes labelled *blow, pluck, shake* and *tap*. Do not leave instruments that are blown in a collection for general use, and tell the children not to put instruments in their mouths if they have been used by other people (unless they have been properly cleaned). This page relates to objectives in the area of *Creative development* (Explore the different sounds of instruments).

Vocabulary: *bang, blow, music, pluck, shake, sound, tap.*

A torch (page 61) introduces a simple electrical circuit. Let the children investigate different types of torch. Ask them in what ways all the torches are similar: they all

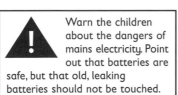
Warn the children about the dangers of mains electricity. Point out that batteries are safe, but that old, leaking batteries should not be touched.

have a bulb, batteries and a switch. Talk about the differences between the bulbs, batteries and switches. The children could take the torches apart to see how they work and explain to the rest of the group how they think the torches work. The others could add their own ideas. Point out electrical sockets in school and ask the children if they know why they should not touch them. Explain that mains electricity is dangerous because it is very powerful, but that batteries are safe because they are not very powerful. The activity on this page could be linked with work in *Communication, language and literacy* (Use talk to

organise, sequence and clarify thinking) and in *Personal, social and emotional development* (Value and contribute to their own well-being).

Vocabulary: *battery, bulb, light, switch, torch.*

Mirror, mirror (page 62) introduces the concept of reflection. The children need plastic mirrors or foil-coated card for safety. You could set up a 'mirror table' on which there are pictures and suggestions for activities: for example, a picture of a snake or a ladder and the challenge 'Make the snake/ladder long', 'Make the snake/ladder short' and even 'Make it disappear'; a picture of an apple with a bite taken from it and the challenge 'Make the apple whole'. Similarly you could provide a picture of a plate or saucer with a piece missing, and ask the children to 'Mend it' using the mirror. Halves of items such as leaves or mats could be completed using a mirror, and objects could be made fatter or thinner. This sheet also focuses on objectives in the areas of *Mathematical development* (Use size language) and *Creative development* (Respond in a variety of ways to what they see).

Vocabulary: *big, half, high, low, mirror, reflect, reflection, small.*

For **A magnet** (page 63), the children will need magnets and a collection of objects to try to pick up: for example, keys; coins; metal, wooden and plastic spoons; stones; shells; tins (with no sharp edges); hinges. Encourage them to try another magnet if the first one they use does not pick up an item. They should notice that some magnets are stronger than others and that some things are not picked up even by a strong magnet. As they become familiar with magnets they could predict before trying to pick up an object. How can they tell if it will be picked up? You could introduce the word *attract*. This page relates to objectives in *Communication, language and literacy* (Extend vocabulary; Use talk to connect ideas, explain what is happening and anticipate what might happen next) and in *Creative development* (Show an interest in what they see and touch; Explore an experience using the senses).

Vocabulary: *attract, magnet, metal, stick.*

Things with springs (page 64) will need springs of different strengths for the children to investigate; these may be obtained from educational suppliers. Also provide toys with

Warn the children not to put their fingers into springs.

springs (and invite the children to bring some in). Talk about 'hidden' springs, such as those in a bed; a piece of an old mattress or sofa could be shown, or a display mattress, armchair or sofa (from a manufacturer) in which the springs are exposed. Take a torch apart and show the children the spring that pushes the batteries onto the metal connector. Also show them the springs under a bicycle seat. Discuss what the springs are for in each artefact and what they are made of. This sheet could be linked with objectives in *Communication, language and literacy* (Extend vocabulary; Use talk to connect ideas, explain what is happening and anticipate what might happen next) and *Creative development* (Show an interest in what they see and touch; Explore an experience using the senses).

Vocabulary: *jump, press, push, spring, squash, squeeze.*

This is me!

- **Finish the picture.**
- **Join the labels to it.**

Make it look like you!

head

arm

leg

My name is _____.

- **Write other labels for your picture.**

Now try this!

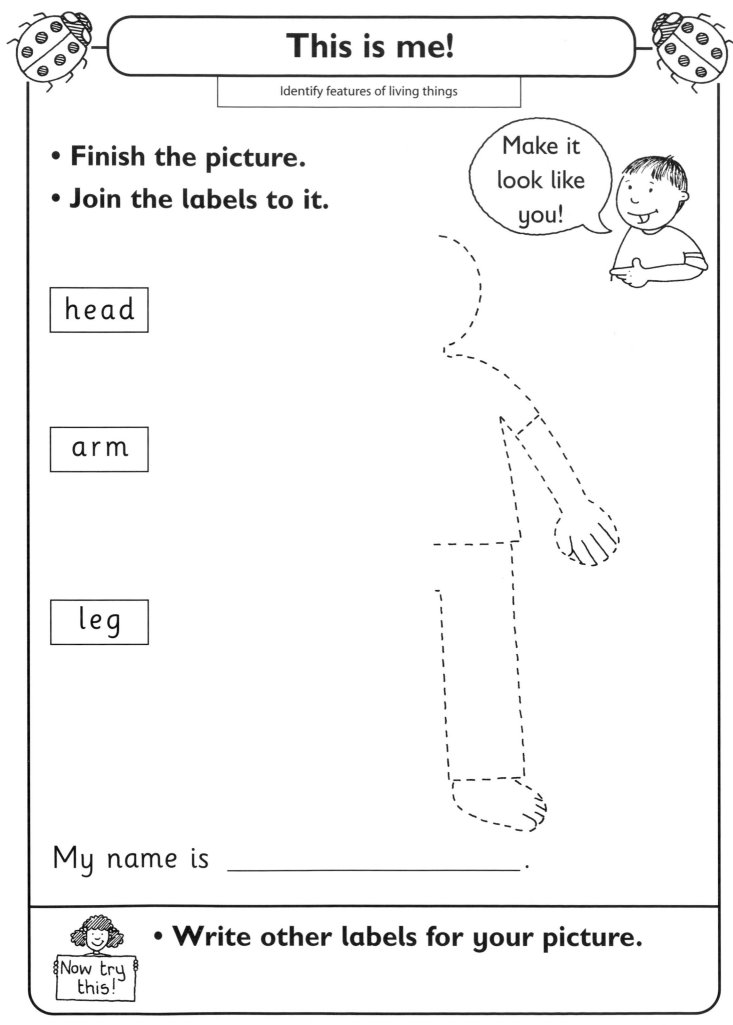

Teachers' note Talk about what the labelled parts of the body are for; ask questions such as 'Why do we have a head?', 'What do we do with our legs?', 'What are our arms for?' In the extension activity, the children could add labels such as *foot*, *hand*, *face* and *knee*. Some children could label other parts of the body: for example, *elbow*, *shoulder*. For children who need more support, an adult could draw the dotted lines to complete the picture and ask the children to trace over them.

**Developing Science
Year R**
© **A & C BLACK**

We are all the same

What do we have?   ✔ or ✗

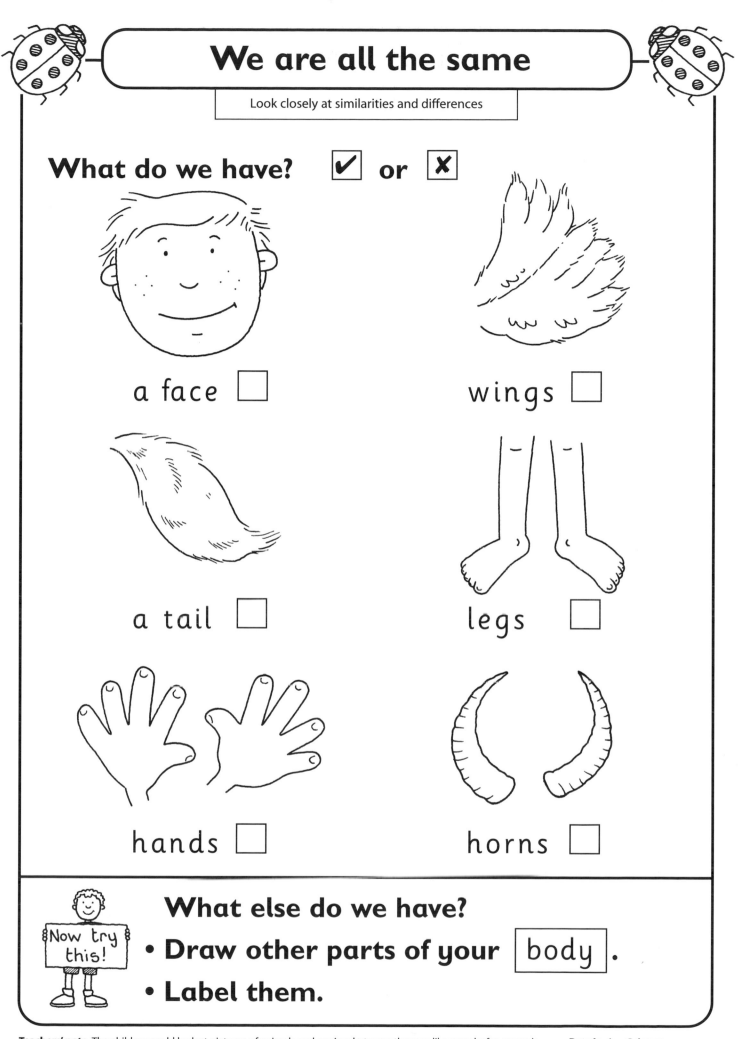

a face ☐

wings ☐

a tail ☐

legs ☐

hands ☐

horns ☐

What else do we have?

Now try this!

• **Draw other parts of your** body .

• **Label them.**

Teachers' note The children could look at pictures of animals and say in what ways they are like people: for example, they have a mouth, eyes, ears, and so on. Ask them how animals are different from people. For children who need more support an adult could point to each picture and ask 'Do you have a …?' Some children could think of other body parts that most people have: for example, arms, feet, fingers. Discuss how people cope if they are injured or disabled.

Developing Science
Year R
© **A & C BLACK**

13

We are all different

- **Look carefully.**

Are they the same **or** different **?**

- **Draw two faces.**
- **Make them** different **.**

Now try this!

Teachers' note Ask the children what it would be like if we all looked the same. How would we know who people were? Ask the children to name ways in which everyone is the same and ways in which we are different. For children who need more support, point to different parts of the faces and ask 'Are their eyes/hair/noses the same?' Some children could cut out faces from magazines and describe how the faces are similar and how they are different.

Developing Science Year R © A & C BLACK

Make a face: teachers' page

Identify features of living things

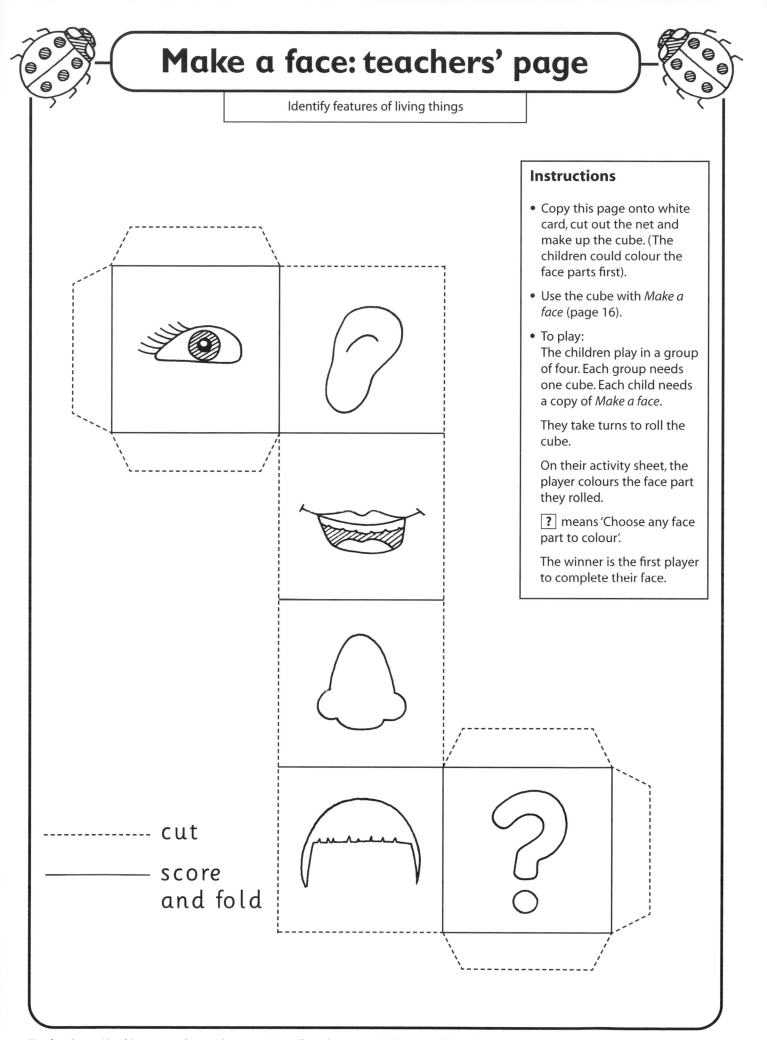

Instructions

- Copy this page onto white card, cut out the net and make up the cube. (The children could colour the face parts first).

- Use the cube with *Make a face* (page 16).

- To play:
  The children play in a group of four. Each group needs one cube. Each child needs a copy of *Make a face*.

  They take turns to roll the cube.

  On their activity sheet, the player colours the face part they rolled.

  ? means 'Choose any face part to colour'.

  The winner is the first player to complete their face.

------- cut

————— score and fold

Teachers' note Use this resource sheet with page 16. You will need scissors and glue. Some of the children could colour the pictures and the net could be laminated to make a re-usable die. Show the children the die and ask them to name the face parts on it. Read the words with them before they play 'Make a face'. Some children could also talk about other parts of the face and contribute to a word-bank about faces: *freckles, nostrils, eyelashes, lips, eyebrows*.

Developing Science
Year R
© A & C BLACK

Make a face

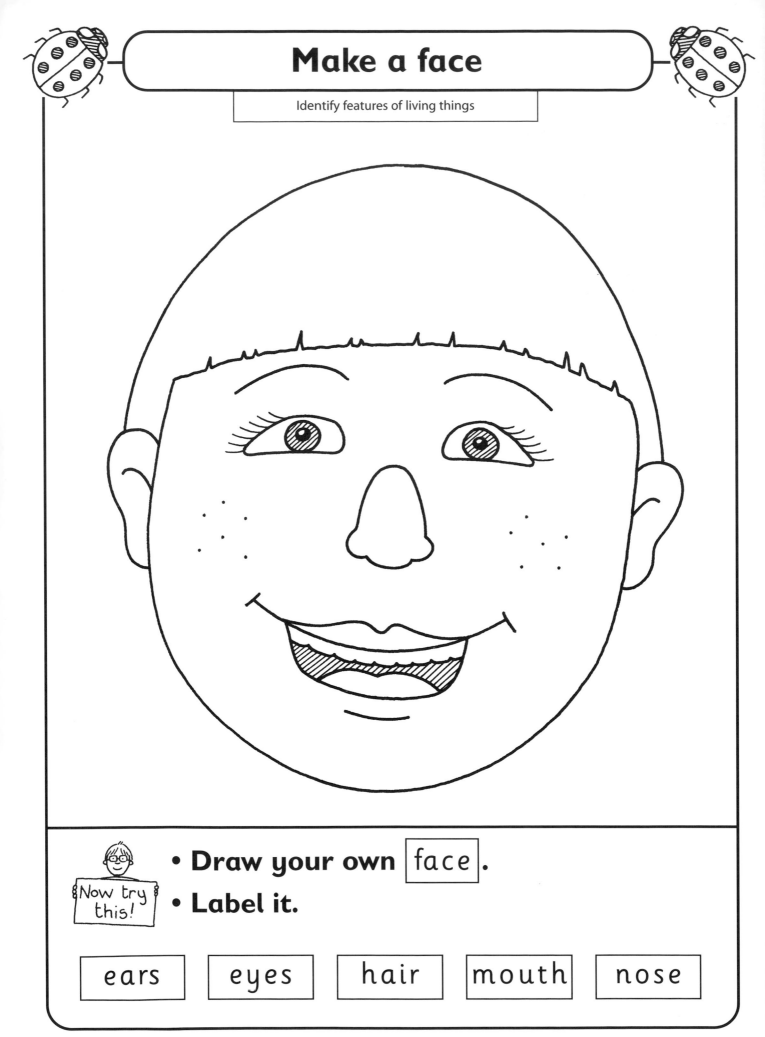

- **Draw your own** face .
- **Label it.**

| ears | eyes | hair | mouth | nose |

Teachers' note Use this with page 15. You could also cut up a copy of the face on this page to make a jigsaw puzzle and ask the children to put it back together. For some children you could cut out faces from magazines, cut them in half vertically, shuffle them and ask the children to match the two halves.

Developing Science
Year R
© A & C BLACK

Eye mask

Find out about features of living things

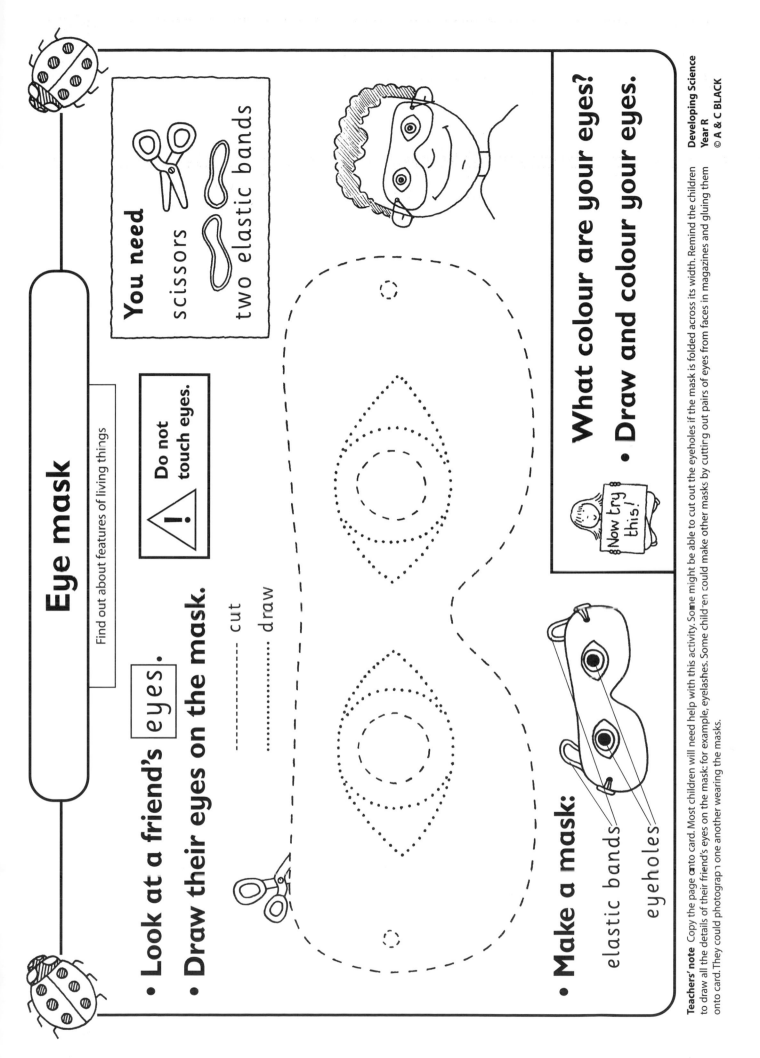

You need

scissors

two elastic bands

⚠ **Do not touch eyes.**

- **Look at a friend's** eyes.
- **Draw their eyes on the mask.**

— — — cut

•••••••• draw

- **Make a mask:**

elastic bands

eyeholes

What colour are your eyes?

- **Draw and colour your eyes.**

Now try this!

Teachers' note Copy the page onto card. Most children will need help with this activity. Some might be able to cut out the eyeholes if the mask is folded across its width. Remind the children to draw all the details of their friend's eyes on the mask: for example, eyelashes. Some children could make other masks by cutting out pairs of eyes from magazines and gluing them onto card. They could photograph one another wearing the masks.

Developing Science
Year R
© A & C BLACK

17

My hands

Examine living things

- **Look at the back of one of your** hands.
- **Draw everything you see.**

- **Write labels.**
- **Join them to your picture.**

finger   hand   nail   thumb

- **Turn the same hand over.**
- **Draw what you see.**

Now try this!

Teachers' note Ask the children to look closely at the backs of their hands. What can they see? Introduce the words for parts of the hand. Ask the children to look at the fronts of their hands. How are they different from the backs? Some children may need to draw round their own hand; others could copy their hand before adding the details. You could give the children pictures of animals that have hands. Ask how they know if they are hands or feet.

**Developing Science
Year R**
© A & C BLACK

My feet

Examine living things

- Look at your [feet] and count your [toes].

Are the pictures right or wrong? [✔] or [✗]

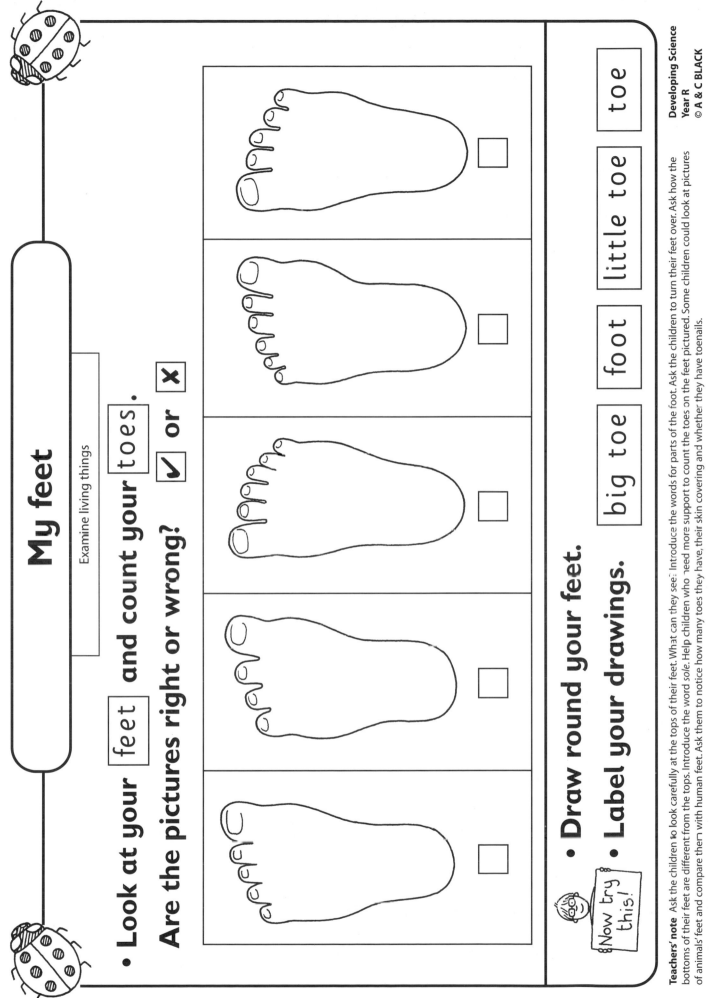

- Draw round your feet.
- Label your drawings.

Now try this!

[big toe] [foot] [little toe] [toe]

Teachers' note Ask the children to look carefully at the tops of their feet. What can they see? Introduce the words for parts of the foot. Ask the children to turn their feet over. Ask how the bottoms of their feet are different from the tops. Introduce the word *sole*. Help children who need more support to count the toes on the feet pictured. Some children could look at pictures of animals' feet and compare them with human feet. Ask them to notice how many toes they have, their skin covering and whether they have toenails.

Developing Science
Year R
© A & C BLACK

See how we grow

- **Cut out the people.**
- **Put them in order.**

| youngest ⟶ | oldest |

- **Draw your family in a line.**

| youngest ⟶ | oldest |

Teachers' note Ask the children how old they think each child in the pictures is. How can they tell? Which one is about the same age as them? Are any the same age as their brothers or sisters? For children who need more support provide pictures of very young and very old people and ask them 'Is he/she young or old?' Some children could cut out pictures of people from magazines and arrange them in age order. Is the biggest always the oldest?

Developing Science Year R
© A & C BLACK

Things I like

Describe features of objects

- **Draw things you like.**
- **Tell a friend why you like them.**

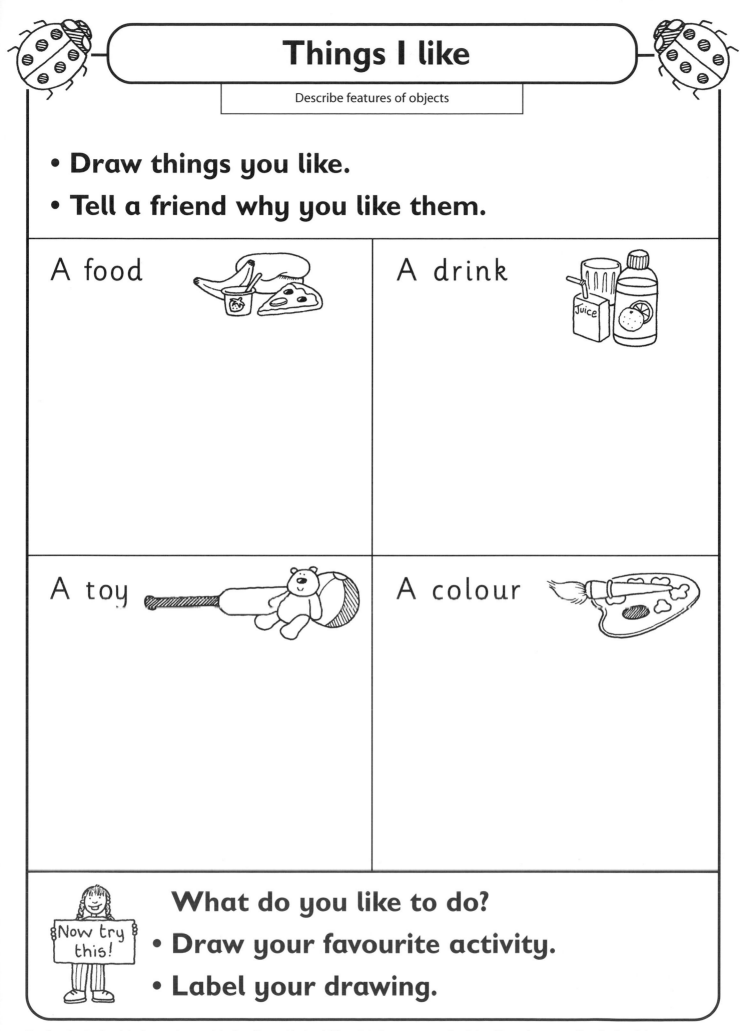

A food

A drink

A toy

A colour

What do you like to do?
- **Draw your favourite activity.**
- **Label your drawing.**

Now try this!

Teachers' note Read the instructions and the headings with the children. Ask them to name a food they like and to describe it: its colour, taste, whether it is soft, hard or chewy, sweet or salty, and so on. Are their favourite drinks still or fizzy? What do they like about their favourite toy? What does their favourite colour make them think of? Some children could bring in information about their hobbies and talk to the class about them.

Developing Science
Year R
© A & C BLACK

Things I can do

Describe simple features of events

What can you do? ✔

☐ cut with scissors	☐ skip	☐ draw
☐ kick a ball	☐ tie shoelaces	☐ swim
☐ ride a bike	☐ hop	☐ fasten a zip

What else can you do?

Now try this!

- **Tell a friend about something else you can do.**

Teachers' note Read the instructions with the children. Ask them what each picture shows, and read the words with them. Ask them if any of them can do the action. They could demonstrate those that are feasible and (verbally) complete the sentence 'I can …' for each picture. This could be linked with setting targets: help the children to choose something they want to learn to do and to think of how they could build up to it in small steps through practice.

Developing Science
Year R
© A & C BLACK

22

Keeping clean

When should you wash your hands?
• Join the pictures to the tap.

What can happen if you don't wash your hands?
• Draw a picture to show what can happen.

Teachers' note Once the children have decided which pictures are connected with washing their hands, introduce the words *before* and *after* and ask the children if they should wash their hands before or after each action, and why. For some children you could cover some of the pictures and concentrate only on either the activities after which they should wash their hands or those before which they should wash their hands, and explain why this is important.

Developing Science
Year R
© A & C BLACK

What can we see?

What can you see in the picture?

baby

ball

bike

bird

car

cat

dog

plane

What can you see in your house?

Now try this!

- **Draw two things in your house.**
- **Label your drawing.**

Teachers' note Before completing the activity sheet, the children could talk about the things they can see in the classroom or outdoors. Ask them to look more carefully, and name some things that are not so obvious. Can anyone else see them? Ask them to circle the objects when they find them in the picture. You could also play 'I spy', inviting the children to name something they can see. Some children could make up their own 'What can we see?' pictures.

Developing Science Year R
© A & C BLACK

What can we hear?

Examine objects and living things using the senses

• **Join the** sounds **to the pictures.**

crack

ding dong

woof

buzz

quack

• **Draw another thing you can** hear **.**
Can you make the sound?

Now try this!

Teachers' note Before completing the activity sheet, the children could talk about the things they can hear in the classroom or outdoors. Ask them to listen more carefully, and name some sounds that are not so obvious. Can anyone else hear them? You could also play an adaptation of 'I spy' ('I hear, with my little ear'). For the activity sheet, it might help some children if they first practise making the appropriate sound for each picture.

Developing Science
Year R
© **A & C BLACK**

25

Loud or quiet?

Sort objects by one criterion

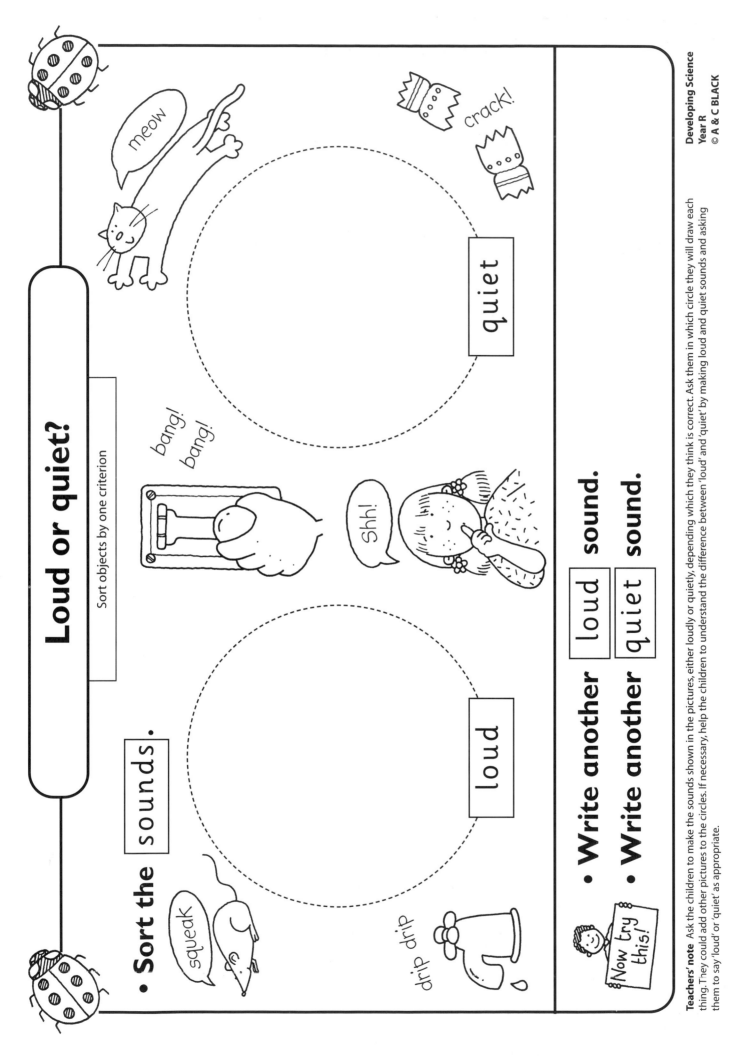

- **Sort the** sounds **.**

meow

crack!

bang! bang!

Shh!

squeak

drip drip

quiet

loud

- **Write another** loud **sound.**
- **Write another** quiet **sound.**

Now try this!

Developing Science
Year R
© A & C BLACK

Teachers' note Ask the children to make the sounds shown in the pictures, either loudly or quietly, depending which is correct. Ask them in which circle they will draw each thing. They could add other pictures to the circles. If necessary, help the children to understand the difference between 'loud' and 'quiet' by making loud and quiet sounds and asking them to say 'loud' or 'quiet' as appropriate.

26

What does it feel like?

Sort objects by one criterion

• **Cross out the things that are wrong.**

soft things

rug   cup   cake

bat   bed   sock

hard things

table   bread   chair

bin   can   cat

Now try this!

• **Find another** soft **thing.**
• **Find another** hard **thing.**

Teachers' note Ask the children to name the objects shown in the pictures; read the words with them. Ask them if the object is soft or hard. Point to the heading and ask if the object should be in that box. If not, they put a cross through the picture. Some children could make a collection of hard things and a collection of soft things and write labels for them.

Developing Science
Year R
© A & C BLACK

Do not touch!

Examine objects using the senses

- **Colour the things you must** not touch .

pencil

light

cooker

teddy

tablets

spoon

knife

book

needle

- **Draw something else you must** not touch .

Now try this!

Teachers' note Ask the children to name the objects shown in the pictures; read the words with them. Ask them if the object is safe to touch. Some children could explain why or why not. You could show them a warning triangle on an empty tablet, medicine or bleach container, and a picture of an electricity warning sign.

Developing Science Year R
© **A & C BLACK**

What can we smell?

What did you [smell]?

- **Colour the picture.**

sticker	flower	crisps	jam	banana
sticker	flower	crisps	jam	banana
sticker	flower	crisps	jam	banana
sticker	flower	crisps	jam	banana

Now try this!

What can you smell at school?

- **Draw two things you can smell at school.**
- **Label them.**

Teachers' note You will need four opaque plastic pots with lids. Put a sticker of a different colour on each pot and stickers of the same four colours on the panels marked 'sticker' on the activity sheet. Prepare pots containing (1) perfumed flower heads or petals, (2) crisps, (3) jam, and (4) banana. Let the children smell each pot in turn and colour the picture of the corresponding object. Warn them not to smell any unknown materials or anything offered by people they do not know.

**Developing Science
Year R
© A & C BLACK**

29

I like this smell

Investigate objects using the senses

- ## Circle the things that smell nice.

- ## Circle the things that do not smell nice.

Now try this!

What is your favourite smell ?
- ## Draw what makes your favourite smell.
- ## Label your drawing.

Teachers' note You could provide a collection of labelled objects and materials for the children to smell and to sort according to whether or not they like them: for example, toast; coffee; hard-boiled egg; cooked cabbage; a carnation, pink, rose, lily of the valley or sweet pea; some jelly; peppermint; chocolate; an old shoe. Some children could talk about the effects of smells: for example, the smells that make them hungry.

Developing Science
Year R
© A & C BLACK

What does it taste like? ICT

Investigate objects using the senses

• **Sort the foods.**

lollipop   chocolate   pizza   crisps

egg   sausage   ice cream   banana

sweet	not sweet

Now try this!

• **Draw another** sweet **thing.**
• **Draw another thing that is** not sweet.

Teachers' note Ask the children to look at the pictures of foods and to name them. Read the captions with them. Ask them if each food is sweet. They should draw the foods (and give them captions) in the correct boxes. Some children could also talk about what makes sweet things sweet: an adult could help them to read food labels and to notice that sweet things often contain sugar.

Developing Science
Year R
© A & C BLACK

My lunch

Understand that good eating practices can contribute to good health

- **Draw some food in the lunch box.**
- **Write the words.**

- **Write your name on the lunch box.**

Now try this!

- **Draw another meal.**
- **Write the word.**

| breakfast | tea | dinner | supper |

Teachers' note Ask the children to name some foods they eat for lunch and to choose the foods they would like for lunch. They should draw the foods in the lunch box and label them. The children will find it helpful to look at the contents of a lunch box to make it easier to draw the foods. If necessary, an adult could write the words for the foods or point them out on food labels.

Developing Science Year R
© **A & C BLACK**

Do not taste!

Investigate objects using the senses

Teachers' note Copy the page onto card and cut out the pictures. Place the pictures face down and invite the children to turn one over. Ask them if they should taste the food or drink; if not, why not? As an extension activity some children could choose one of the things they should not taste and tell or write a story about someone who tasted it.

Developing Science
Year R
© A & C BLACK

33

Around our school

• **Colour these things that you see outside.**

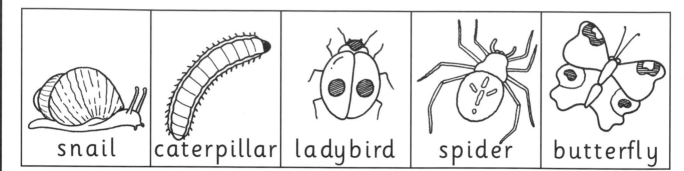

| snail | caterpillar | ladybird | spider | butterfly |

• **Circle them in this picture.**

• **Draw an animal that lives outside your home.**

• **Label your drawing.**

Now try this!

Teachers' note Ask the children to look at the pictures of animals and to name them; read the captions with them. Ask them how the animals are similar to, and different from, one another. You could help by asking questions such as 'Does it have a shell?', 'Does it have legs?', 'How many legs does it have?' and 'Does it have wings?' If necessary, begin by showing the children colour photographs of animals and asking them to point out the legs, wings and so on.

Developing Science Year R
© A & C BLACK

Leaf match

Look closely at similarities and differences

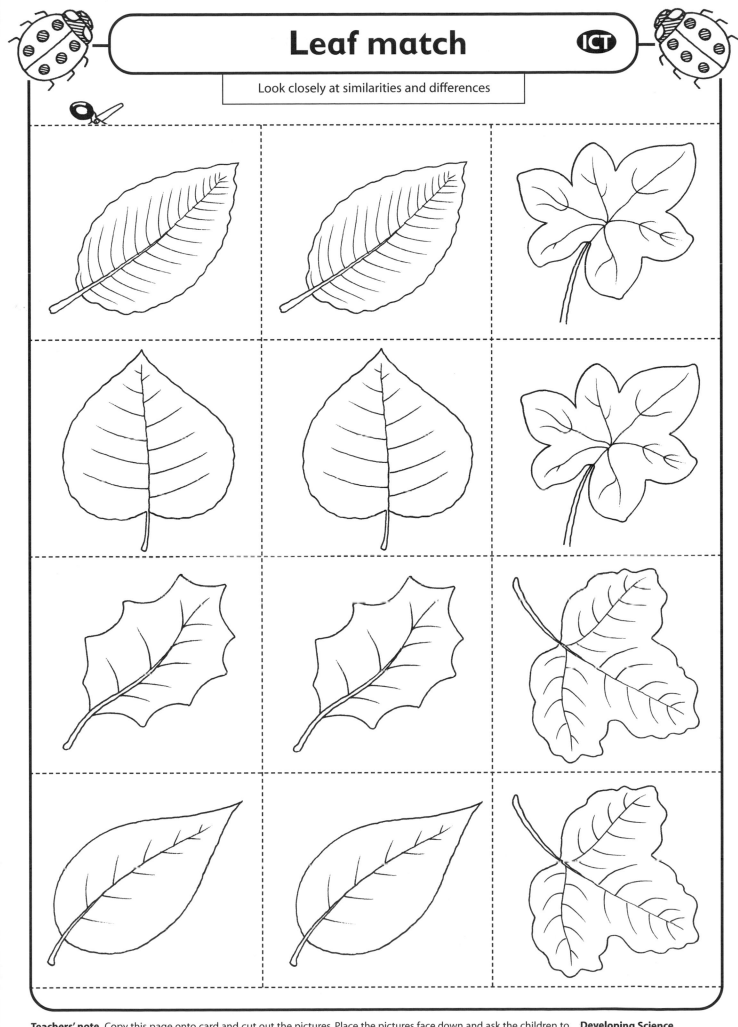

Teachers' note Copy this page onto card and cut out the pictures. Place the pictures face down and ask the children to take turns to turn over two cards. Are they the same? If so, they keep them; if not, they turn them back over. The winner is the one who has the most cards when all have been turned over. Some children might need help distinguishing between the leaves: ask them if they have one point or lots of points, if they are short or long, fat or thin.

Developing Science
Year R
© **A & C BLACK**

35

At the park

Talk about what is seen

What did you see in the park? ✔

dandelion ☐

duck ☐

grass ☐

holly ☐

daisy ☐

sparrow ☐

spider ☐

squirrel ☐

tree ☐

Now try this!

What else grows **in the park?**
- **Draw another plant from the park.**

What else lives **in the park?**
- **Draw another animal from the park.**

Teachers' note This page can be used for recording some of the things observed during a visit to a park. Encourage helpers to record (in writing or on cassette) any living things the children notice. Tell them the names of any they do not know and talk about their distinctive features, such as shape, colour and pattern. Back at school, ask the children what they can see in the pictures and read the captions with them. Ask them to tick only the ones they saw in the park.

**Developing Science
Year R
© A & C BLACK**

Look closely at patterns

• **Finish the pictures.**

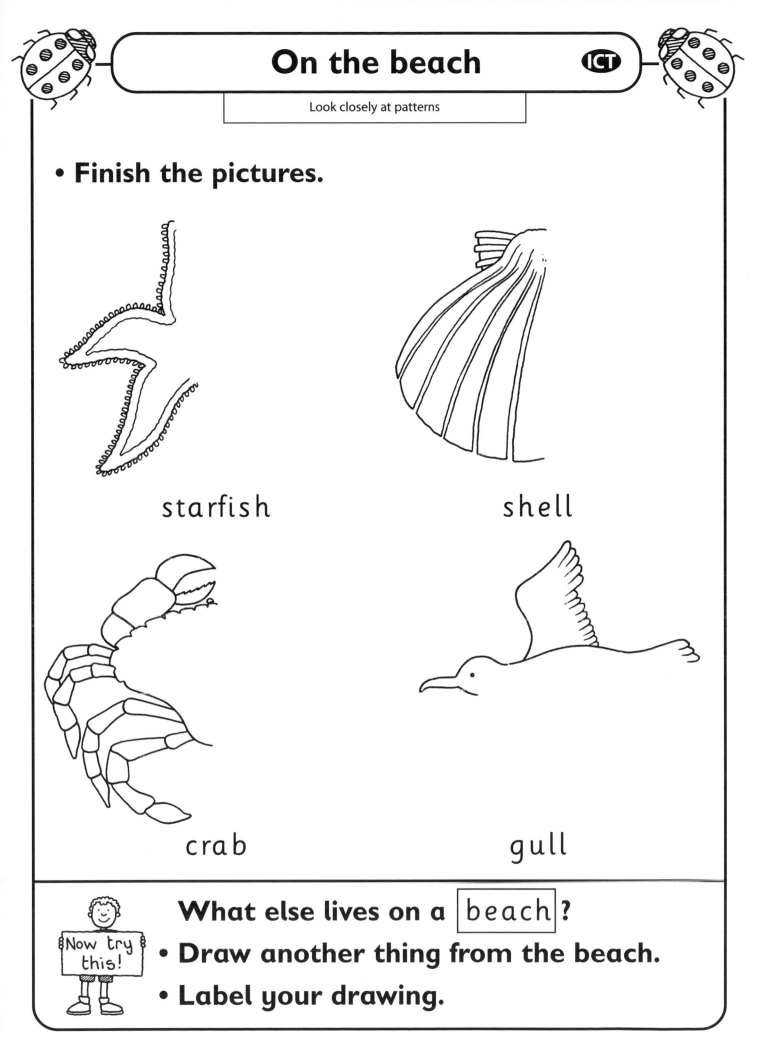

starfish

shell

crab

gull

What else lives on a beach **?**

• **Draw another thing from the beach.**

• **Label your drawing.**

Now try this!

Teachers' note Provide colour pictures of a starfish, a cockle shell, a crab and a gull. If possible, it is also useful to show the children a picture of a beach with these on it. Ask the children where on the beach they might find them: in the water, in the air, on the sand, on a rock, or in many different places. Discuss the shapes and patterns the children can see on each animal; they could count its legs, claws, wings or tentacles.

**Developing Science
Year R**
© A & C BLACK

At the zoo

Where do the animals live?

- **Write** land **or** water .

shark

zebra

snake

goldfish

- **Draw another** land **animal.**
- **Draw another** water **animal.**

Teachers' note Ask the children to name each animal in turn and where it lives. They could name other land and water animals and talk about what would happen to the land animals if they were put in water and to the water animals if they were kept out of water.

Developing Science
Year R
© A & C BLACK

Animal jigsaw

Look closely at similarities and differences

• **Cut out the pieces.**

• **Make the animals.**

• **Write captions.**

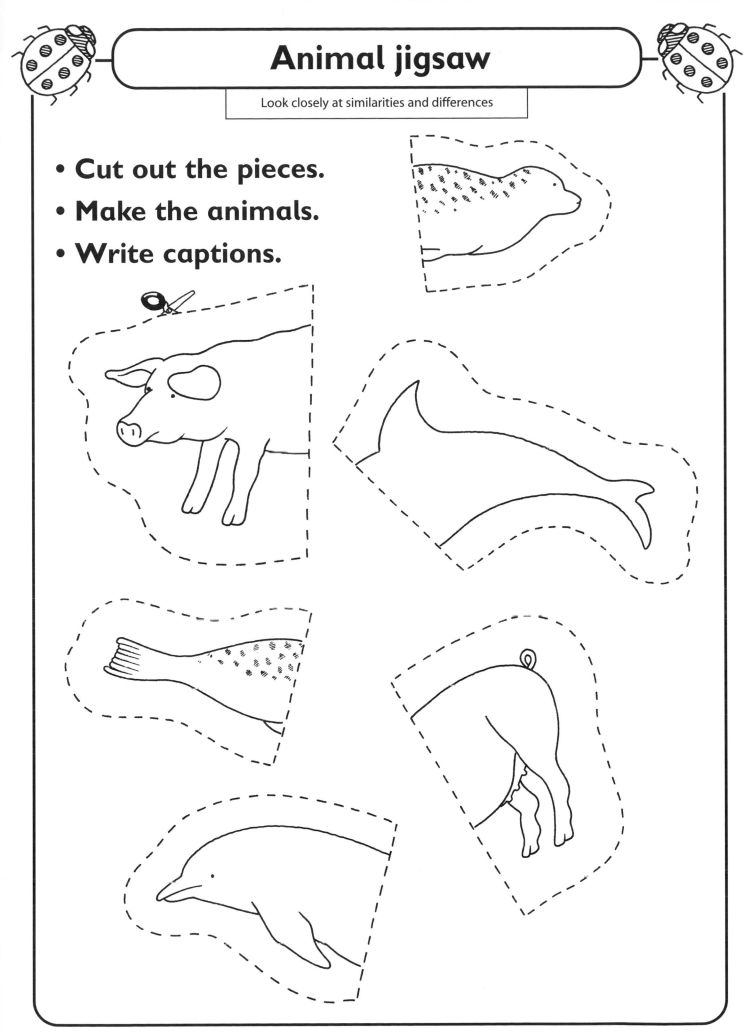

Teachers' note Ask the children to cut out the halves of animals and fit them together to make the whole animals. What animals are they? The children could glue them onto another sheet of paper and write a caption for each picture. Some of them could also write about what the animal looks like: for example, 'This is a pig. It has four legs. Its feet are called trotters.'

Developing Science
Year R
© **A & C BLACK**

Who is my mum?

Examine living things

• **Join the** young animals **to their mothers.**

caterpillar

tadpole

frog

hen

chick

butterfly

• **Draw another young animal with its mother.**

Now try this!

Teachers' note Begin by pointing out that every animal (including people) has a mother. The children might be able to talk about the mothers of some of their pets. Ask the children to look at the pictures and name the animals. Read the words with them; they could also copy the words. The children could draw lines to link the young animals to their mothers or cut them out and glue them in pairs onto another sheet of paper.

**Developing Science
Year R**
© **A & C BLACK**

How do they move?

How do the animals move **?** ✔

bird	fly	
	hop	
	swim	
	walk or run	
fish	fly	
	hop	
	swim	
	walk or run	
rabbit	fly	
	hop	
	swim	
	walk or run	
cat	fly	
	hop	
	swim	
	walk or run	

Now try this!

• **Draw an animal that slides or wriggles.**

Teachers' note Ask the children how they can tell from the pictures how the animals can move; they should notice features such as legs, large feet, fins and tails. Tell them that they can tick more than one box if the animals can move in more than one way: for example, it might be able to hop and walk or run. They could collect other examples, including some that can walk or run and swim (for instance, ducks).

Developing Science
Year R
© A & C BLACK

What do they eat?

ICT

Examine living things

- **Draw some animals.**
- **Write their names.**

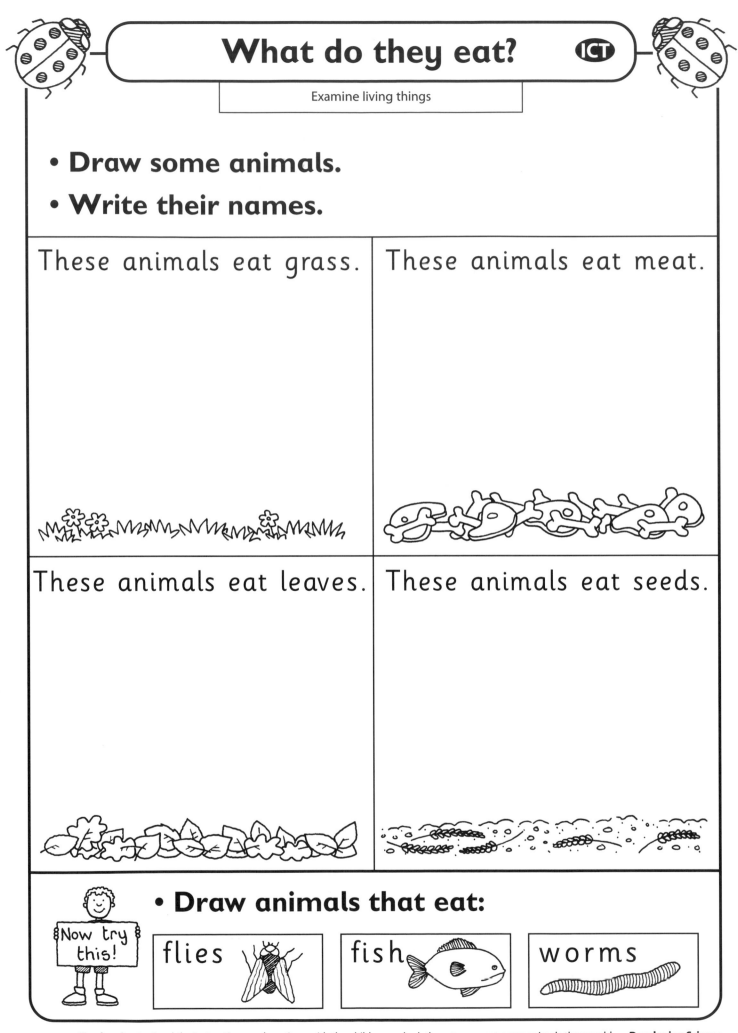

These animals eat grass.

These animals eat meat.

These animals eat leaves.

These animals eat seeds.

Now try this!

- **Draw animals that eat:**

flies

fish

worms

Teachers' note Read the instructions and captions with the children and ask them to suggest some animals they could draw in each set. Help them to draw on previous learning (for example, from visits or videos). You could ask them what the different animals they saw at the park or at the zoo were eating.

Developing Science
Year R
© **A & C BLACK**

A bird

- **Watch a** bird **.**
- **Tick what it does.** ✔

perch ☐

fly ☐

walk ☐

hop ☐

drink ☐

sing ☐

Now try this!

- **Draw another thing the bird does.**
- **Write a label.**

Teachers' note This page could be used while the children are observing birds (see page 9). If they are familiar with local birds, some children could watch one type of bird, such as the bluetit, starling or sparrow. If the children are not sure of the meanings of the words for the actions, use a model bird (for example, a Christmas tree decoration) and make it perform different actions. Ask the children what it is doing.

Developing Science
Year R
© A & C BLACK

A snail

Examine living things

ICT

- **Finish the picture.**
- **Join the labels to the picture.**

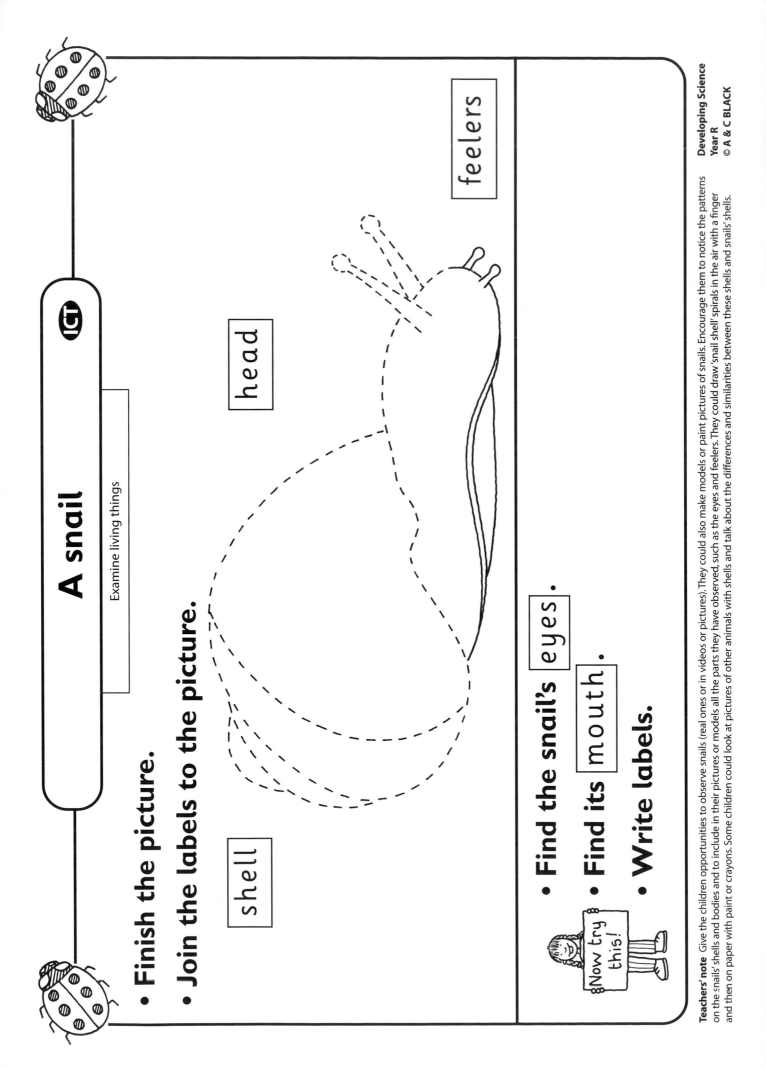

head

feelers

shell

- **Find the snail's** eyes **.**
- **Find its** mouth **.**
- **Write labels.**

Now try this!

Teachers' note Give the children opportunities to observe snails (real ones or in videos or pictures). They could also make models or paint pictures of snails. Encourage them to notice the patterns on the snails' shells and bodies and to include in their pictures or models all the parts they have observed, such as the eyes and feelers. They could draw 'snail shell' spirals in the air with a finger and then on paper with paint or crayons. Some children could look at pictures of other animals with shells and talk about the differences and similarities between these shells and snails' shells.

Developing Science
Year R
© A & C BLACK

44

Sand

Examine materials

What can you do with ⟨dry⟩ sand?

What can you do with ⟨wet⟩ sand? ✔ or ✘

pour

dry ☐   wet ☐

build

dry ☐   wet ☐

draw

dry ☐   wet ☐

sieve

dry ☐   wet ☐

Now try this!

• **Tell a friend what you know about** ⟨dry sand⟩ **and** ⟨wet sand⟩.

Teachers' note The children first need to have handled and talked about wet and dry sand and noticed the differences between them (see page 9). Read the instructions with the children and help them to read the captions. Invite those who completed the extension activity to say what they know about wet and dry sand; ask the others to contribute. You could make a display about wet and dry sand: the differences, how they behave and what each can be used for.

Developing Science
Year R
© A & C BLACK

Water

Examine materials

What can you do with water ? ✔ or ✘

pour ☐

build ☐

draw patterns ☐

squirt ☐

drink ☐

dig a hole ☐

What else can you do with water?

Now try this!

- **Tell a friend.**
- **Try it out together.**

Teachers' note Use this page to help the children to record their observations about water. Some children will need an adult to supply the vocabulary they need and to ensure that the children understand it. After the activity you could provide some ice, and ask the children how it is different from water. They could complete the activity sheet again, for ice instead of water.

**Developing Science
Year R**
© **A & C BLACK**

Are they waterproof?

Investigate materials using the senses

You need

water   gloves   cotton

bowl   rubber   wool   plastic

• Do this:

Is your hand dry?

Are they [waterproof] ?   ✔ or ✖

plastic ☐

rubber ☐

cotton ☐

wool ☐

Teachers' note Tell the children that they are going to test some materials to see if they are waterproof (see page 9). Provide examples of the gloves and ask the children to point out the ones made of plastic, rubber and so on. Which do they think will be waterproof? Ask them to look at the pictures at the top of the page and invite them to read the words, if they can. Ask them what they need and what they have to do. How will they know if the glove is waterproof?

Developing Science
Year R
© A & C BLACK

Hot, warm, cold

• **Join the pictures to the word** hot , warm **or** cold .

iron

cola

ice

ice cream

hot

warm

cold

toast

cat

light

fire

• **Draw other things that are:**

Now try this!

hot   warm   cold

Teachers' note Ask the children if they know what each picture shows; read the words *hot, warm* and *cold* and the words for the objects with them. Ask them to draw lines to join each picture to one of the words in the circles. To help some children to read the words *hot, warm* and *cold* they could colour the circles red, orange and blue respectively. Some pictures may be able to be joined to more than one word.

**Developing Science
Year R
© A & C BLACK**

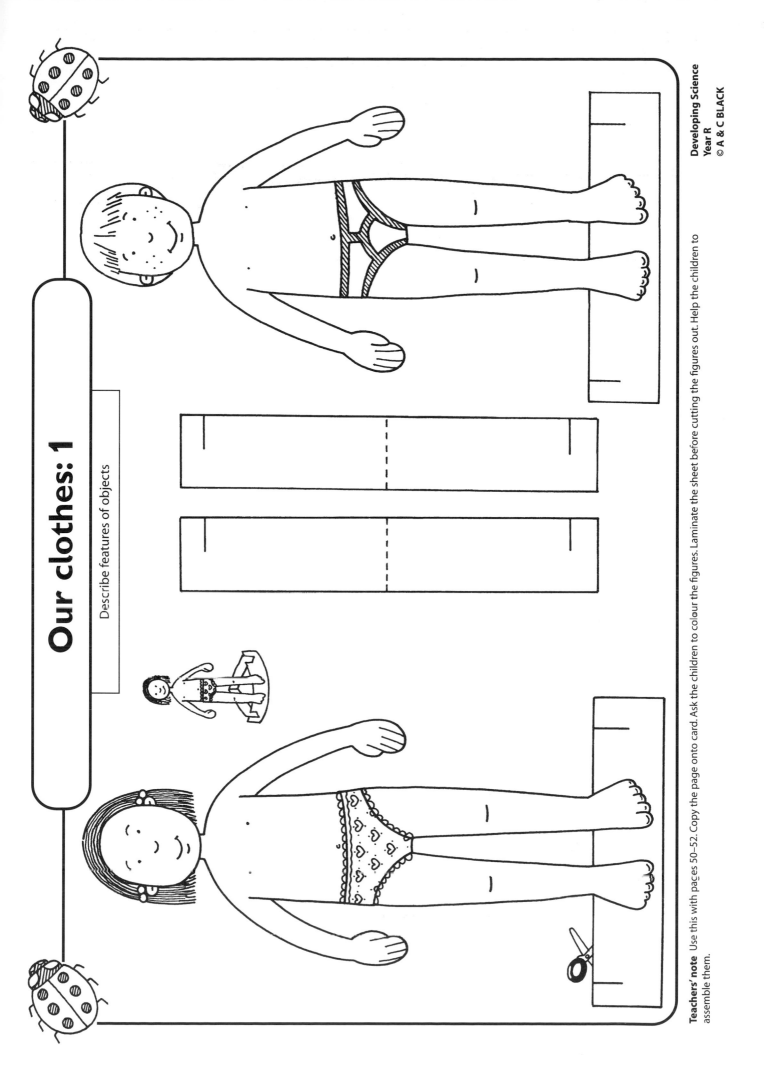

Our clothes: 1

Describe features of objects

Teachers' note Use this with paces 50–52. Copy the page onto card. Ask the children to colour the figures. Laminate the sheet before cutting the figures out. Help the children to assemble them.

Developing Science
Year R
© A & C BLACK

49

Describe features of objects

Teachers' note Use this with pages 49 and 51–52. Copy the page onto card. Ask the children to colour the clothes. Score along the fold lines of the tabs before cutting the clothes out ready for the children to dress the figures.

**Developing Science
Year R**
© **A & C BLACK**

Our clothes: 3

Describe features of objects

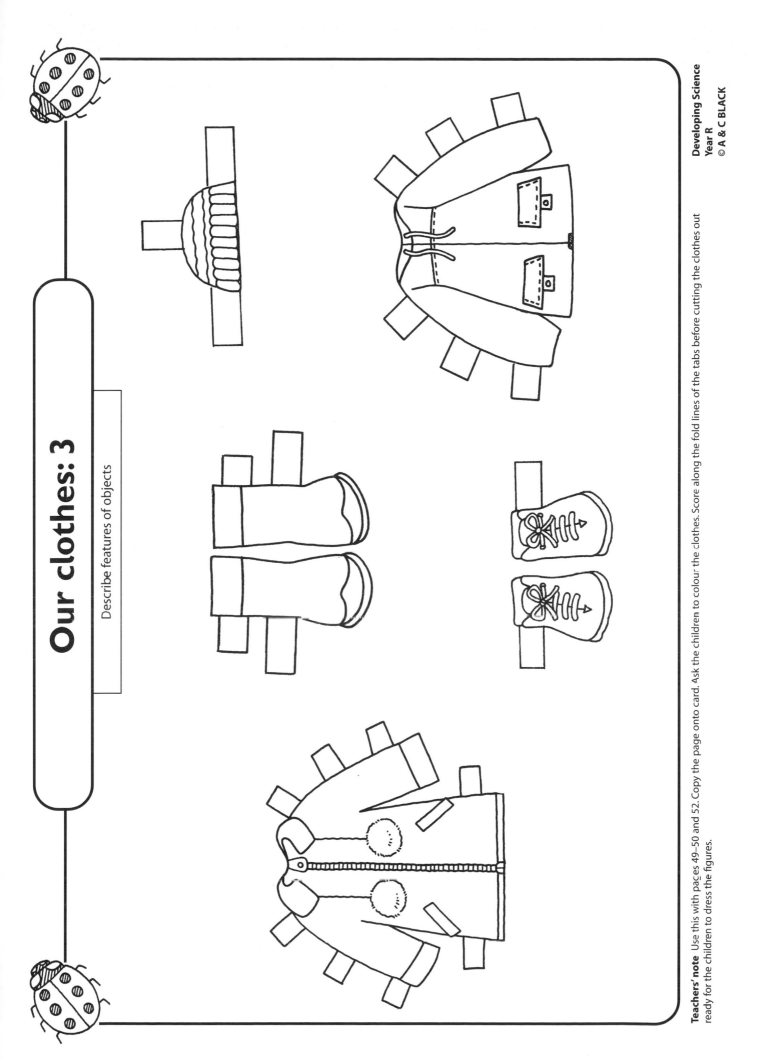

Teachers' note Use this with pages 49–50 and 52. Copy the page onto card. Ask the children to colour the clothes. Score along the fold lines of the tabs before cutting the clothes out ready for the children to dress the figures.

Developing Science
Year R
© A & C BLACK

Our clothes: 4

Describe features of objects

Teachers' note Use this with pages 49–51. Copy the page onto card. Ask the children to colour the clothes. Score along the fold lines of the tabs before cutting the clothes out ready for the children to dress the figures. As an extension activity, some children could tell a story about a little boy or a little girl who went out wearing the wrong clothes for the weather and what happened to him or her.

Developing Science
Year R
© A & C BLACK

Rough or smooth?

Look closely at similarities and differences

• **Write** rough **or** smooth .

window

mat

_____

_____

spoon

book

_____

_____

brush

brick

_____

_____

Now try this!

• **Draw two other** rough **things.**
• **Draw two other** smooth **things.**

Teachers' note Provide examples of the objects shown in the pictures and ask the children first to predict if they will be rough or smooth and then to find out; they can then record their findings on this page.

Developing Science
Year R
© A & C BLACK

Squashy stuff

Look closely at similarities and differences

Which things are squashy **?**
Which things are not squashy **?**

sponge	blocks	book
bat	pillow	pencil
teddy	stone	rag doll

- **Draw two other** squashy **things.**
- **Label them.**

Now try this!

Teachers' note Provide examples of the objects shown in the pictures and ask the children first to predict whether or not they will be squashy and then to find out; they can then cut out the pictures and glue them onto another piece of paper (in two circles labelled *squashy* and *not squashy*). Some children could make up a song about squashy things in which each line begins 'I squashed a … and …' (they describe what happened).

**Developing Science
Year R**
© **A & C BLACK**

Shine on

- **Look at things at school.**

  Are they shiny **?** yes **or** no

  scissors

  paint

  block

  sand

  water

  mirror

- **Look at some** shiny **things.**

  Which ones can you see your face in?

Now try this!

Teachers' note Provide examples of the objects shown in the pictures and ask the children first to predict if they will be shiny and then to find out; they can then record their findings on this page. Ask the children about the feel of shiny things (they are smooth). Ask them for the opposite of *shiny*; introduce the word *dull*. Some children could choose materials with which to make mirrors and then test their mirrors. Do they work as well as real mirrors? If not, why not?

Developing Science
Year R
© A & C BLACK

Toy cars

What makes toy cars go?

- **Choose a toy car.**
- **Draw it in the correct box.**

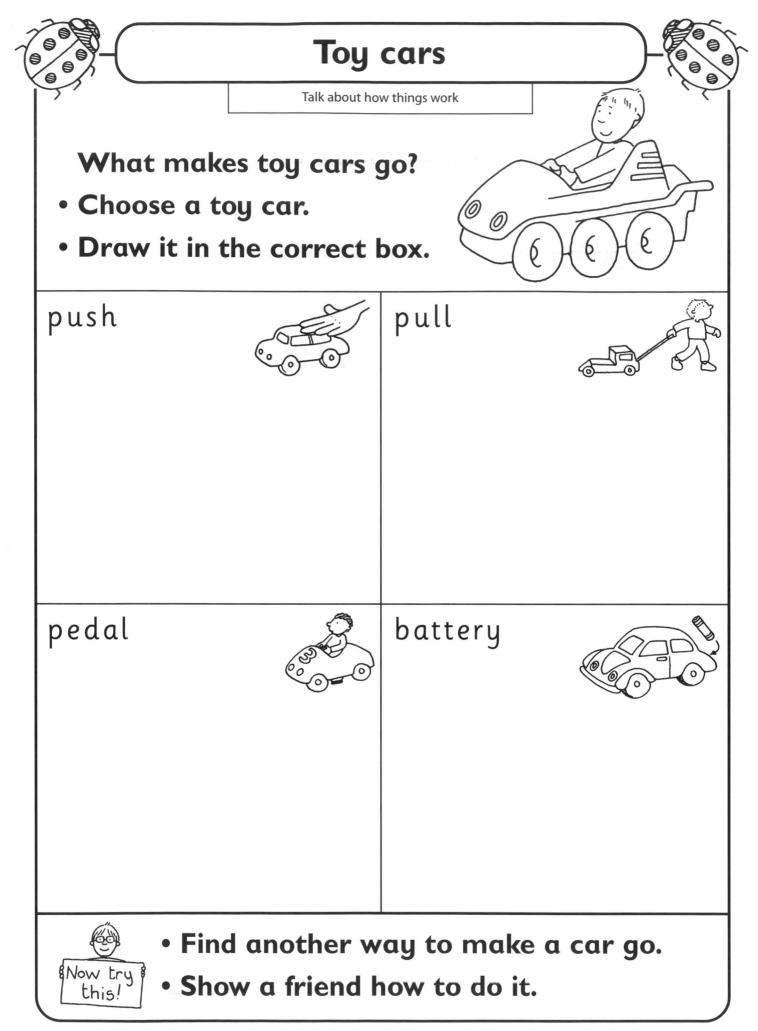

push	pull
pedal	**battery**

- **Find another way to make a car go.**
- **Show a friend how to do it.**

Now try this!

Teachers' note The children will need a collection of toy cars. They can use this page to record the findings of their investigations into what makes the cars go. Some of them might also be able to identify other ways of making toy cars move: for example, clockwork or friction motor.

Developing Science
Year R
© **A & C BLACK**

Boats

Talk about how things work

What makes boats go?

- **Draw the boats.**

rowing	wind	motor

- **Look at some toy boats.**
- **Find something else that makes them go.**

Now try this!

Teachers' note Show the children real boats on videos and in pictures. Let them play with model boats in a water tray. Talk about what makes boats go. The children can use this page to record their observations of real boats. Some of them might be able to think of other ways in which boats are made to move: for example, steam (or other types of engines), pedals or paddle-wheels.

Developing Science
Year R
© A & C BLACK

Wheels

Talk about how things work

- **Find the** wheels .
- **Colour them.**

- **Look around for other things with wheels.**
- **Draw another thing with wheels.**
- **Write a label.**

Now try this!

Teachers' note Ask the children to find the wheels and colour them. Encourage them to talk about the vehicles and other artefacts on which they spot the wheels. You could introduce the word *vehicle* and make word-banks of words for wheeled vehicles. The children could also design and make small toy cars from cardboard boxes. Discuss how to attach the wheels; draw attention to the fact that they must be able to turn.

**Developing Science
Year R**
© A & C BLACK

Turn, turn, turn

Talk about why things happen

• **Colour the** handles **you turn.**

⚠ **Take care. Keep your fingers safe.**

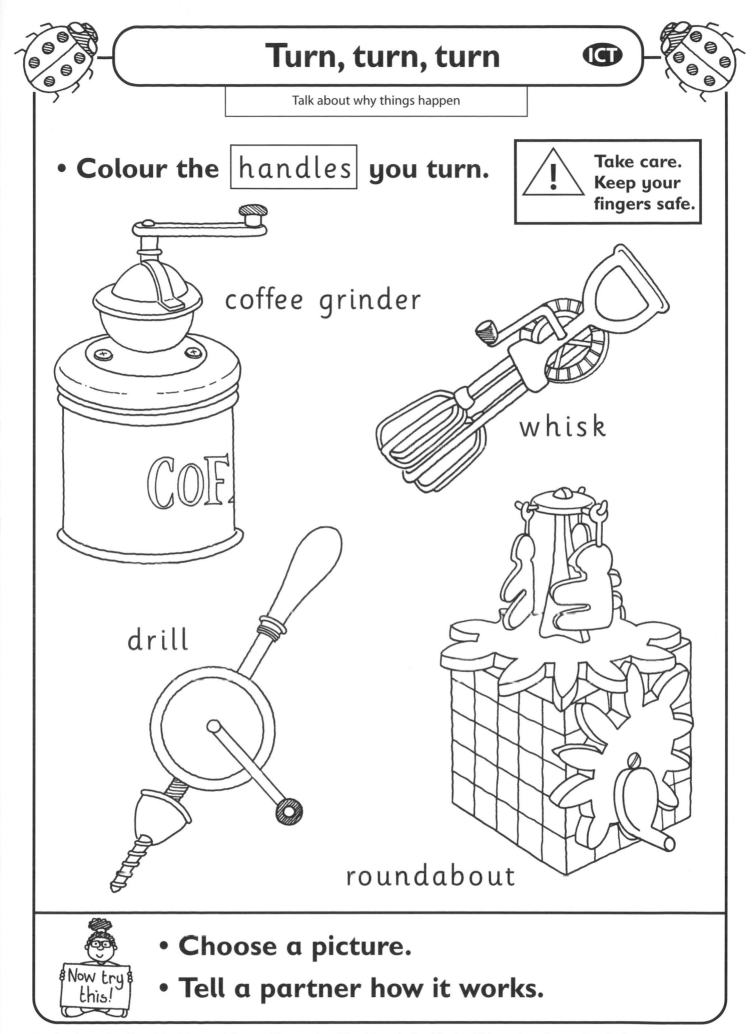

coffee grinder

whisk

drill

roundabout

• **Choose a picture.**
• **Tell a partner how it works.**

Now try this!

Teachers' note For this activity, it is essential to provide examples of the objects depicted for the children to investigate. (The construction material is Start Gear). Encourage the children to talk about what happens when they turn the handles. You could point out the different directions in which the different wheels on an artefact turn and how they fit into one another to make this happen. Some children might be able to make model machines with wheels.

Developing Science
Year R
© **A & C BLACK**

59

Music makers

Ask questions about how things work

- **Draw some music makers.**
- **Write labels.**

I tap these.

I shake these.

- **Find another kind of music maker.**
- **What do you do to make a** sound ?
- **Draw it and write:** I _____ this.

Now try this!

Teachers' note Provide a collection of musical intruments for the children to explore. Enlarge this page to A3 and use it for the children to record their observations of musical instruments. You could make another copy with the headings in the circles changed to *I blow these* and *I pluck these*. Invite the children to talk to the class about an instrument they have played. Ask the children questions about how the instruments make sounds and encourage them to ask their own questions.

Developing Science
Year R
© A & C BLACK

A torch

Ask questions about how things work

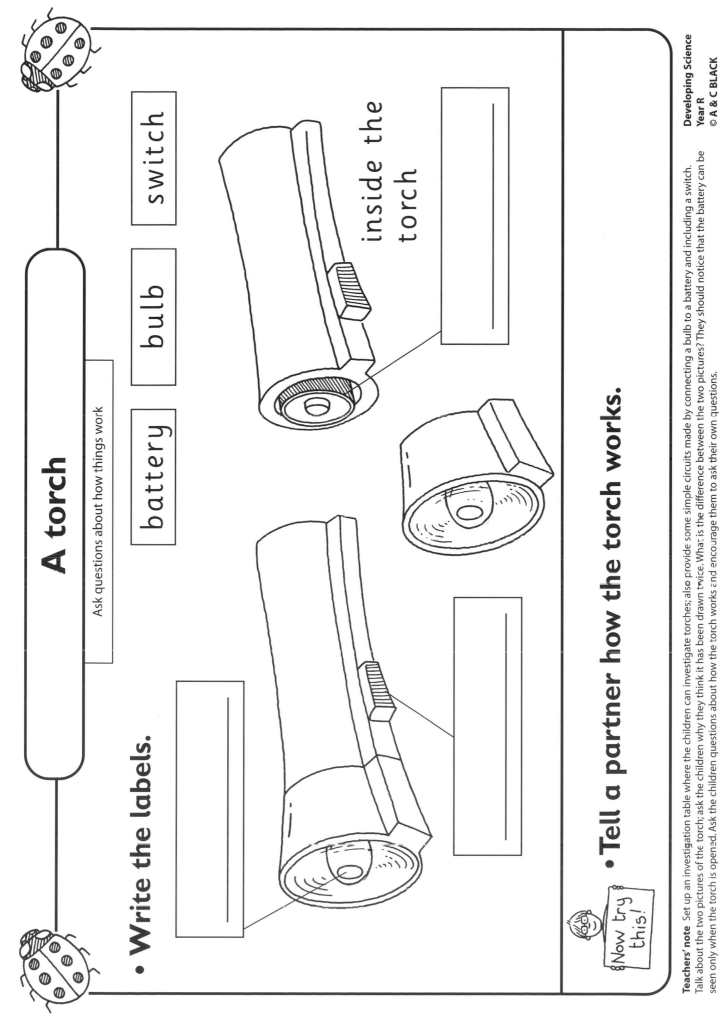

| battery | bulb | switch |

inside the torch

• Write the labels.

• Tell a partner how the torch works.

Now try this!

Teachers' note Set up an investigation table where the children can investigate torches; also provide some simple circuits made by connecting a bulb to a battery and including a switch. Talk about the two pictures of the torch; ask the children why they think it has been drawn twice. What is the difference between the two pictures? They should notice that the battery can be seen only when the torch is opened. Ask the children questions about how the torch works and encourage them to ask their own questions.

Developing Science
Year R
© A & C BLACK

61

Mirror, mirror

Investigate objects using the senses

- **Stand a** `mirror` **on the pictures.**

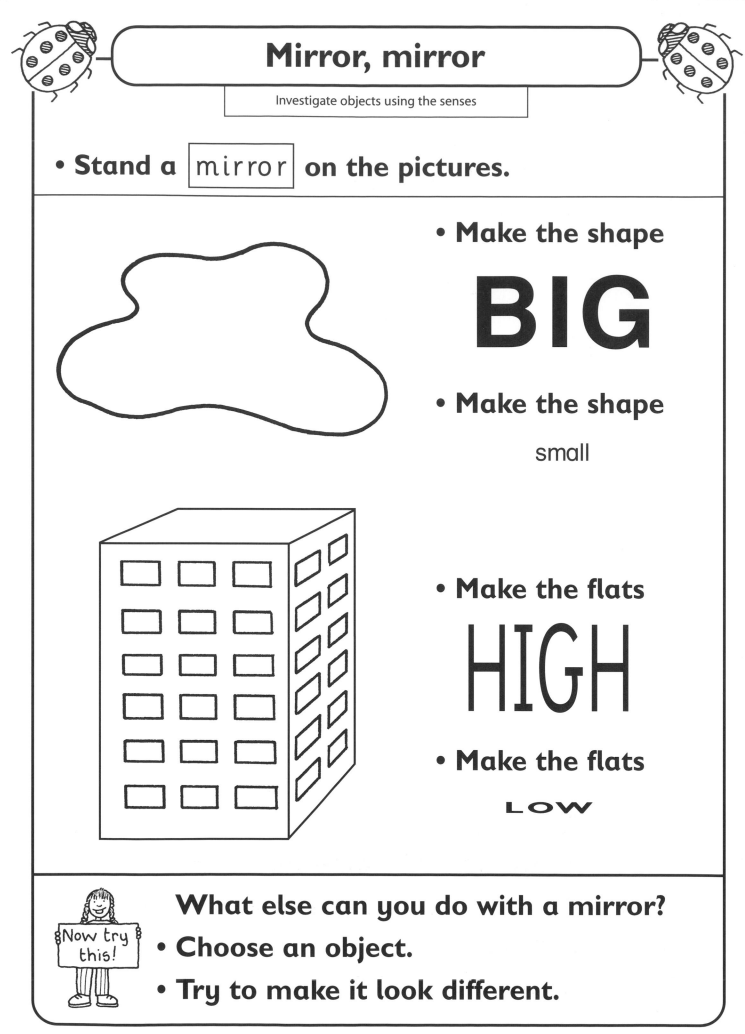

- **Make the shape**

BIG

- **Make the shape**

small

- **Make the flats**

HIGH

- **Make the flats**

LOW

What else can you do with a mirror?

Now try this!

- **Choose an object.**
- **Try to make it look different.**

Teachers' note Set up an investigation table where the children can investigate mirrors (see page 11). Invite them to talk about what happens as they move the mirror in different directions. Encourage them to use directional language such as *up, down, sideways, backwards, forwards, right* and *left*.

**Developing Science
Year R**
© **A & C BLACK**

What does a magnet pick up?

- Draw the things.

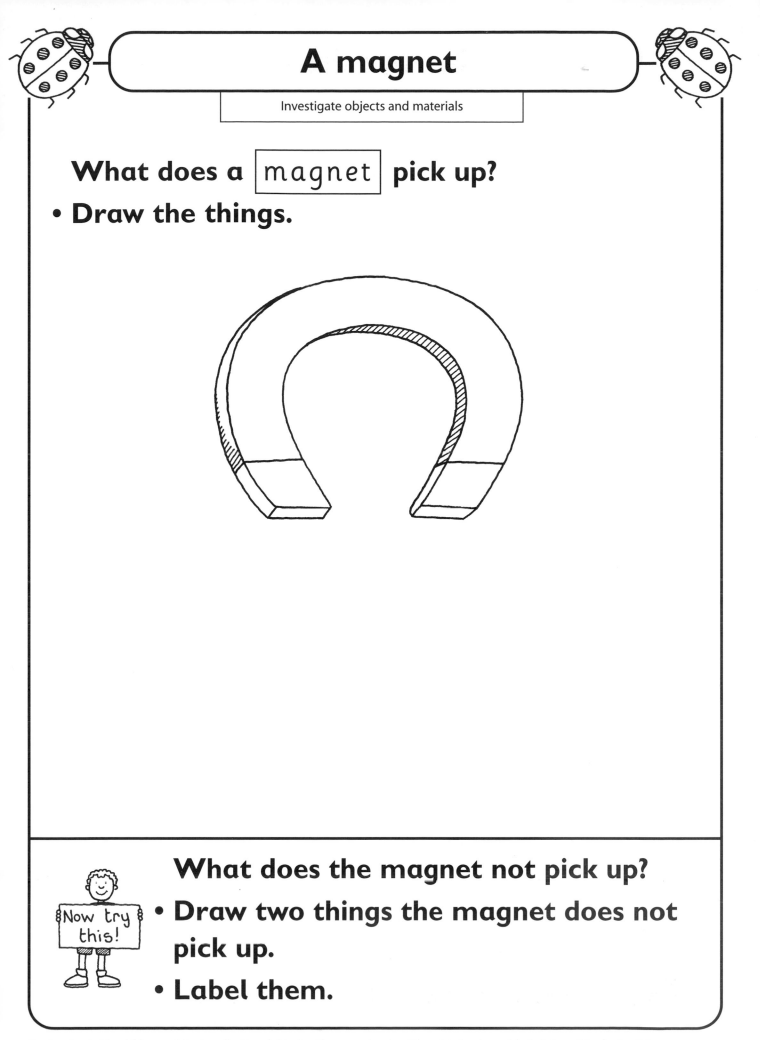

What does the magnet not pick up?

- Draw two things the magnet does not pick up.
- Label them.

Now try this!

Teachers' note The children could test a collection of objects with a magnet and sort them into two boxes labelled ✔ and ✘ to show whether or not they were picked up by a magnet. Talk about what the objects are made of and what this has to do with whether they are picked up. Some children might need practice in identifying metals. Point out that they are hard and they feel cold. Draw attention to the sound they make when tapped.

Developing Science Year R © A & C BLACK

Things with springs

Ask questions about how things work

Do they have springs? ✔ or ✘

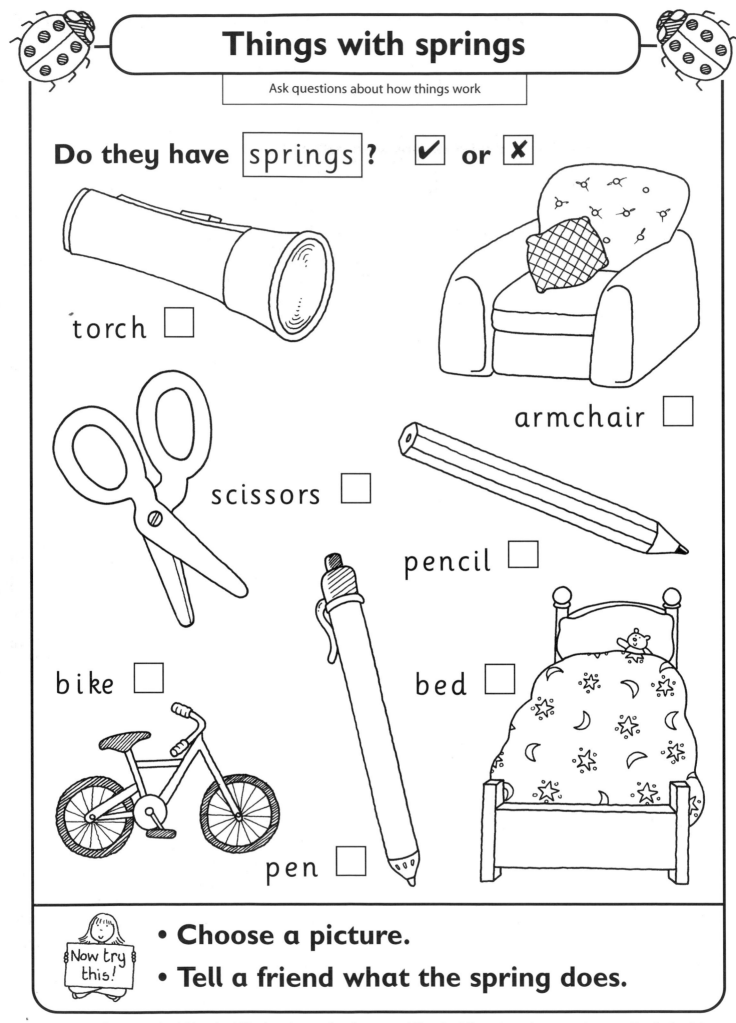

torch ☐

armchair ☐

scissors ☐

pencil ☐

bike ☐

bed ☐

pen ☐

- **Choose a picture.**
- **Tell a friend what the spring does.**

Teachers' note The children should first investigate springs (see page 11). They should learn that springs can make things jump and they are used for pushing things and for making things soft and comfortable. To help the children to understand the meaning of 'spring' they could pretend to be springs during a PE lesson. Ask them to pretend to be small springs inside pens and big springs inside mattresses.

Developing Science
Year R
© A & C BLACK